MANAGEMENT QUESTIONS

JOHN LOK

Copyright © John Lok
All Rights Reserved.

This book has been published with all efforts taken to make the material error-free after the consent of the author. However, the author and the publisher do not assume and hereby disclaim any liability to any party for any loss, damage, or disruption caused by errors or omissions, whether such errors or omissions result from negligence, accident, or any other cause.

While every effort has been made to avoid any mistake or omission, this publication is being sold on the condition and understanding that neither the author nor the publishers or printers would be liable in any manner to any person by reason of any mistake or omission in this publication or for any action taken or omitted to be taken or advice rendered or accepted on the basis of this work. For any defect in printing or binding the publishers will be liable only to replace the defective copy by another copy of this work then available.

Contents

Preface   v

Prologue   vii

1. Management Define   1

2. Partnership Define   8

3. Nuke Mission Strategy   13

4. The Difference Between Internal And External Stakeholders   20

5. Limited Company Strategies   25

6. Swot Analysis   33

7. Internal And External Growth   37

8. Change Management   43

9. Globalization   48

10. Human Resource Management   52

11. Delaying   59

12. Communication   66

13. Leadership Style   72

14. Motivation   77

15. Organizational Culture   82

16. Organizational Agreement   88

17. Crisis Management   94

18. Company Define   100

19. Finance Define   107

20. Loan Finance   113

21. Budget   119

Contents

22. Business Cooperation Advantage ... 125

23. Asset Define ... 129

24. Manufacture Management ... 136

25. Product Innovation ... 141

26. Management Calculation ... 145

27. Production Methods ... 150

28. Quality Ensure Measurement ... 155

29. Joint Venture ... 160

30. Innovation Advantages ... 167

31. Capacity Increasing Methods ... 172

32. Private Limited Companies Strategies ... 179

33. Diseconomic Of Scale ... 184

PREFACE

Introduction

Any organizations must need to learn how to implement the most suitable management strategy in order to achieve their organizations effectively. I shall attempt to explain the basic management strategy to define in order to let readers can have more understanding whether what the actual management strategy mean.

Prologue

Table of content

Chapter 1 Management define p.3-7

Chapter 2 Partnership define p.8-13

Chapter 3 Nuke mission strategy p.14-19

Chapter four The difference between internal and external stakeholders p.20-25

Chapter five Limited company strategies p.26-30

Chapter six SWOT analysis p.31-34

Chapter seven Internal and external growth p.35-39

Chapter eight Change management p.40-44

Chapter nine Globalization p.45-49

Chapter 10 human resource management p.50-54

Chapter 11 Delaying p.55-58

Chapter 12 Communication p.59-62

Chapter 13 Leadership style p.63-67

Chapter 14 Motivation p,68-72

Chapter 15 organizational culture p.73-77

PROLOGUE

Chapter 16 Organizational agreement p.78-82

Chapter 17 crisis management p.83-88

Chapter 18 Company define p.89-92

Chapter 19 Finance define p.93-96

Chapter 20 Loan finance p.97-100

Chapter 21 Budget p.101-104

Chapter 22 Business cooperation advantage p.105-107

Chapter 23 Asset define p.108-112
Chapter 24 manufacture management p.113-115
Chapter 25 product innovation p.116-119

Chapter 26 Management Calculation p.120-124

Chapter 27 production methods p.125-128
Chapter 28 Quality Ensure Measurement p.129-133

Chapter 29 Joint venture p.134-138
Chapter 30 Innovation Advantages p.139-142

Chapter 31 Capacity Increasing Methods p.143-147

Chapter 32 Private Limited Companies Strategies p.148-152
Chapter 33 Diseconomic of Scale p.153-156

I

Management define

Q1a. Definition of entrepreneur

A business is any organization that uses resources to meet the needs of customers by providing a

product or service that they demand. Entrepreneur means an organizer who creates some

new events, organizes factors of production, undertakes risk and handles economic uncertainty

involved in new enterprise/venture. Any entrepreneur has to perform a number of functions

as a vital factor of production.

For example, Jessica wants to start a resume writing service

business who owns these personal characteristics, as hard work, desire for high

achievement, highly optimistic, independence, foresight, good organizer, innovative, time management, effective communication, analytical ability, independence.

As Jessica is an entrepreneur who may include idea generation and scanning of the best

suitable idea, determination of the business objectives, production analysis and market

research, determination of form of ownership/organization, raising necessary funds,

recruitment, making change and business operation for whose resume writing service.

Q1b. Definition of tertiary sector business

Tertiary sector business activity firms that provide services to consumers and other businesses,

such as retailing, transport, insurance, banking, hotels, tourism and telecommunications, even

including information technological service providers.

Primary sector consists of agriculture, secondary sector is formed by industry and the

tertiary sector is incorporating all other activities that did not fit in first two sectors. For example,

Jessica's business would provide a resume writing service to individuals. Thus, the tertiary sector includes

activities such as trade and domestic activities as well as health, education ,research and development.

The four attributes that are common to service tertiary sector activities include simultaneity

between production and consumption, product intangibility, interactivity between producer and

customer/user and the idea of non-stock.

This characteristics are due to the nature of the services as a work in process, so products are generated by the tertiary sector which may be tangible or intangible and both physical as well as

information service tertiary sector.

Q1c. Definition of finance set up

Capital consists of finance needed to set up a business any pay. For its continuing operations as

well as the man made resources used in production. These include capital goods, such as computers,

machines, factories, offices and vehicles.

Start up finance means entrepreneur gives whose cash to set up whose business capital

to operate for any business in the beginning. It is sourced either by sole trader or partner's cash or

bank loan or corporation's shares issued capital from shareholders. For example, Jessica buys office

equipments for her resume writing business or gym instructor buys gym sport equipments for

his gym sport service centre business.

Q1d. Definition of capital equipment

Business input of capital equipment is such as computers, machines, printers etc office equipments.

Some firms are capital intensive that is electricity power supply business has a high proportion of capital

equipment to other factors of production . e.g. power station. For example, the gym instructor would

need gym equipments and Jessica needs a computer in office.

Capital equipment presents tangible and fixed assets in any organizations. It means

the tangible items which are to permanently serve the business process. Capital equipment can be consumed in one accounting period and generally are depreciated over a number of years.

Durable means of production are caused by capital equipment. During its useful life, it gives

off a flow of different usages (e.g. plant equipment). The capital equipment characteristics

include organizational assets are used to supply business operations. Examples include

production line for manufacturing, testing equipment used by a construction company.

Capital equipments are typically high cost, infrequent purchases, that requires good

decision making to minimize long term costs.

Q2. Outline of production factors of production needed to set up the business providing to

school leavers.

For this resume writing service to school leavers business of Jessica, its factors of production

may include that the entrepreneur (capital) uses to pay office rent, electricity, water, buying office equipments,

printers and computers and stationary etc general office operational expenditure ; (land) she rents

an office or may work at home to let every school leaver to know where who can give individual working

experiences and educational background information to Jessica to help them to write individual resume;

(labour) Jessica can choose either to work for herself or she can employ employees to assist her.

employing writing resume skilful writers will be intangible asset if who can help her to attract many school

leavers. Instead of employing writing resume assistant, Jessica could also employ cleaner, office receipt, accounting clerk staffs if she needed.

Finally, the factor of production includes Jessica is a (enterpriser) herself who needs to manage and control

and give ideas how to operate her writing resume service business efficiently and effectively every day.

Q3. Business functions of gum instructor's business

I recommend that gym instructor's gym sport service centre business ought include these departments:

(a) Marketing department can research different gym sport service competitors' prices to measure

what service fee charging is the most reasonable service fee. It aims to compare their gym sport service quality,

the satisfactory level of clients' feeling to play sport bicycles and running machines etc equipment and

gym instructor serving attitude to get the most reasonable service fee. Marketing department can design

the suitable different payment plans to provide clients to choose payment methods.

After clients use gym sport bicycles and running machines etc equipments from gym instructors

instruction, who can choose either to pay service fee per hour or choose to join to be monthly or

annual member to pay discount service fee. Thus, I recommend who need to employ at least one

market research staff to research the competitors' different service quality and every client

satisfaction level to evaluate what is its reasonable price every month.

(b) Finance department can record and analyse his gym business accounting financial information. For example: Purchasing sport bicycles and running machines etc sport

centre equipments expenditure, staff salary, rent, electricity, water, insurance etc expenditure.

(c) Human resource department can identify the work force needs, recruits, selects and trains appropriate staff.

For example, employing at least one gym service manager gym instructor or gym instructing trainee, cashier,

cleaner positions when his business expands.

(d) Customer service department can help every individual to register member record, cashing, answering

enquiry etc front line service in gym sport service centre.

(e) Operating management department can manage gym sport service operation to ensure to satisfy individual

need successfully.

Q4. Explain reasons why most enterprisers choose to set up the tertiary sector business

Enterprisers prefer to choose to set up tertiary sector business. The reasons are as below:

Firstly, Developed countries is declining in the importance of secondary sector activity and an increase in the

tertiary sector. It is known as deindustrialisation. Rising incomes associated with higher living standards

have led consumers to spend much of their extra income on services rather than more goods.

These developed countries' people need more entertainment to become their social habits.

Thus, hotel, travel, restaurant, cinema, music, internet etc entertainment tertiary sector businesses

will increase demand in these developed countries.

Secondly, Manufacturing workers may find it different to find employment in other sector of industry and it

causes structural unemployment. Manufacturing businesses in the developed countries face much more

competition and these competitors tend to be more efficient and use cheaper labour. Moreover,

technological innovation causes new technological products import demand increasingly. For example, laptop

computers, desk computers, mobiles etc high technological products will increase demand because developed

countries' people have afford money to buy these products commonly. It rises import and domestic secondary

sector firms have been forced to close.

Thirdly, enterprisers don't require large amounts of capital to buy capital equipments if who choose to

do tertiary sector service or trading businesses.

Finally, some enterprisers rely on their past tertiary sector business experience own skills and interest.

Thus, It implies entrepreneurs have more opportunities to choose to set up service or trading tertiary sector

businesses in any developed countries market nowadays.

II

Partnership define

Q1 Explains the term of partnership

A partnership is a collaborative relationship between two or more people to work toward shared objectives

through a mutually agreed division of labour. Partners can deliver of practical solutions at the strategic level

to carry on business together, with shared capital investment and usually shared responsibilities.

The characteristics of partnership include a shared leadership among individuals who are empowered

by own organizations and trusted by partners to resolve conflicts, a shared common vision and purpose

that recognizes value contribution of all members and acceptance of differences (e.g. values, ways of

working) is key components of a successful partnership.

Q2 Outline two benefits to Larry Page and Sergey Brin of starting Google as a partnership.

The two benefits to Larry Page and Sergey Brin of starting Google as a partnership include these

two hands.

They can exchange their individuals with networking skills, sharing information, coordinating efforts,

transferred or combined service and governance and resources to concentrate on managing themselves

internet commerce field to operate partnership together. Hence, they can achieve strategic alliance benefit of

decision making power is shared or transferred. Management of a program or mutual interest to participating

organizations' missions to reduce risk by one internet technological firm itself.

The another hand, their business losses can shared and additional capital can injected by each partner to have

enough capital to expand their internet technological business in the short term.

Q3 Examine the difficulties the partners would have encountered when they set up Google.

The difficulties the partners would have encountered when they set up Google which can include these two

factors of external competitive environment and internal organization cooperation factors.

On the internal organization cooperation factor, they can exist different vision and ideas to operate whether

one partner dominates or partners compete for the lead, lack of understanding role and responsibilities and lack

of support from partner organizations with decision making power and difference of philosophies and manners

of working and lack of commitment and unwilling participants and financial and time commitment outweigh potential benefits and too little time for effective consultation and spending much time to get trust to build long

term partnership relationship and employees need time to adapt new organizational culture and change

management between of them during they set up Google in the beginning together.

For example problems include that design company logo and administration and managing employee

cooperation and deciding what users are looking for from their websites and how to calculate page's room

housed in their servers and how to make users spend as little time as possible on their website search etc

problems. When they set up Google internet technological business in the beginning.

On the external competitive environment factor, it faced the Yahoo internet technological monopoly.

It provided email service, news headlines, a website directory, advertisement, webpage hosting and

other online services to different countries. Yahoo sources of revenue include sale of

advertisement space, paid premium, content and extended service commission for sale made through

its online stores and park link placement. Hence, these two partners set up partnership which need have

unique internet service to win their this Yahoo competitor in this internet commerce market in the beginning.

Q4 Explain the term public limited company (plc).

Public limited company is incorporated legal form of organization to run business. Companies are incorporated to form an entity with a separate legal personality. This means that the organization can do

business and enter into contracts in its own name.

A public limited company is owned by its members (shareholders), who have invested in the business and

enjoy limited liability. For example, the company's finances are separate from the personal finances of owners.

It has legal right to sell shares to the general public. Its shard price is quoted on the national stock exchange.

Q5 Discuss the advantages and disadvantages to Google following its conversion to a plc in 2004.

Although, Google changed to public limited company form from partnership in 2004 and it's revenue

sources must not be changed after 2004. Generally, Google drives its revenue for two sources: Sale of its

research technology to other companies and sale of advertisement space on its search result pages.

However, it will still have advantages and disadvantages to a public limited company in 2004.

It's advantages include it was a partnership and it can't issue shares to public to increase capital before. After

2004, it formed a public limited company, it can ease of buying and selling of shares for shareholders to

encourage investment and access to substantial capital sources due to the ability to issue a prospectus to the

public and to offer shares for sale, public limited company can have separate legal entity and limited liability to

Google.

Otherwise, public limited company also have these

disadvantages include it needs legal formalities in

formation, cost of business consultants and financial advisers when creating it, share prices subject to

fluctuation, sometimes for seasons beyond business's control from poor economy, legal requirements

concerning disclosure of information to shareholders and the public, e.g. annual publication of detailed report

and accounts, risk of takeover due to the availability of the shares on the stock exchange and directors

are influenced by short-term objectives of major investors.

III

Nuke mission strategy

Q1 Explain the reason for Nike, Inc. having a mission statement

A mission statement is a statement of the organization's purpose, what it wants to accomplish in the larger environment.

The reasons for Nike , Inc needs a mission statement as below:

(a) Nike, Inc. is a sport products trading company. it needs have a clear mission statement because

Nike, Inc. can know what it's business is, who it's clients are, what clients value do and what it's

business should be these questions to achieve its business intention more successful if it had a clear mission

statement . Thus, its stakeholders can know core purpose and activity in a short paragraph.

For example, it's mission statement is to bring inspiration and innovation to every athlete in the world of whose every body and who can become athlete successfully.

(b) The reason for it needs have a mission statement include it can give message to let Nike's clients and

employees to know what it's products can attribute in global sport product market, it should be translated into

supporting objectives for each level management and create a hierarchy of objectives that are consistent with

one another within organization, Nike's objectives are followed the mission statement. All mission statement

can influence it's objective can be achieved. Thus, it can recognise the markets and benefits of serving

these sport markets.

(c) It can give ethical reference to motivate employees by identifying positive core goals.

Q2 Analyze two strategic objectives that Nike, Inc. might try to achieve.

Nike, Inc was formed as an importer of Japanese shoes, 1962. Today, Nike was holding a global market

share of approximately 37% (Puma.com) In the United States, it's sport products were sold through

about 22,000 retail accounts; world wide, it's products were sold in more than 160 countries. It developed

to sell of athletic footwear, apparel and equipment, which together approximately $18,6 million in sales

during Nike's 2008 year. It divided its products into four segments: footwear, apparel, sport equipment and

other products. In 2008, these segments accounted for 52%, 28%, 6% and 14% of Nike's revenue

respectively (Adidas Group.com). In addition to manufacturing sportswear and equipment, it operated

retails stores the Nike town name. Nike's competitors, like New Balance, but also against large athletic
footwear and manufacture like Adidas AG and Puma. Thus it implied Nike had good strategic planning
to achieve it's sale objective before.

However, I think Nike should have these problems which would encounter in the future. For example,
although Nike always represents high quality and highly reliable. However, the cost will be higher than other
brands. The public feels that Nike overcharges its consumers and should reduce the price of their products
and it had any new sport products to develop because clients' taste are varied from time to time and it's
sport products' life cycle are getting short and clients can have a wide range of selection from running
shoes or sunglasses with Nike brand in the future and fake products could be one of the most critical
reasons for Nike. In fact, in some Asia countries: Taiwan, China or Vietnam. Nike could lose more than
million dollars because they don't have effective way to stop those take products.
There should be specific , measurable, achievable, realistic and time specific and should be based on the
corporate aims.

However, I shall recommend these two strategic objective that Nike, Inc. might try to achieve.
Strategic planning means the process of developing and maintaining a strategic fit between the
organization's goals and capabilities and its changing marketing opportunities.

The first strategic objective , it can raise sales by 5% by end of the year. It's methods can include that

Nike might try to analyze it's current business portfolio of sport running shoes and sport equipments etc

products to judge different countries' clients' number of age group segments to buy their different product

numbers in the future. This strategic objectives is to create value for Nike Inc. clients and build clients

relationship by market segmentation and targeting.

Hence, on the strategic level, Nike Inc. might design business portfolio in its strategy. Business portfolio

is the collection of businesses and products that make up it. Thus, Nike Inc. must analyze its

current business portfolio or strategic business units and decide which strategic business units

should receive more or less or should downsize its business portfolio by eliminating some style of

sport running shoes and equipment etc products designs of business units that are not profitable

or that no longer fit Nike's overall strategy.

Another method include that differentiation is creating superior customer value by actually differentiating the

market offering and positioning is arranging for a product to occupy a clear, distinctive and desirable place

relative to competing products in the minds of target consumers.

Nike might try to diversify to produce more new style and design sport running shoes and new sport

equipments product numbers to attract more clients to choose to buy its sport products. This market strategy is

differentiation and positioning in global sport product markets, aim to win its competitors. For example: Old styles in new colour athletic running shoes.

The another strategic objective, Nike can achieve all new sport products developed during the year

should use materials from natural sources and it can carry out an environmental audit of the sport

product range by the end of the year.

Its methods can include that Nike can cut greenhouse gas emissions by 10% in all factories by the end

of year and all new sport products developed during the year should use materials from natural sources or

renewable resources and use suppliers who are socially responsible and implementation of the common

high standards for the wellbeing of all employees. For example, giving fair salary to factories workers,

willingness to pay cost of environment protection and establishment and implementation of ethical codes

of practice to become a socially responsible organization.

Reference

Financial reports (2009), PUMA.com, http://about.puma.com/EN/5/35/35/.

Income statement (2009), Adidas Group, http;//adidas-group.corporate-publications.com/en/group-management-report/income-statement-7.html.

Q3 Using Nike, Inc. as an example, outline the main components you might expect to see in its

environment audit.

Nike, Inc.'s factories need have safety and clean working environment for their workers to work

and reduce air and water pollution to natural environment from its plastic wastage to damage natural environment to influence different countries stakeholders of citizen health.

Its plastic wastage pollution level is very serious to influence the manufacturing countries

stakeholders of citizen health daily. Hence, its environment audit needs outline these main components

as below:

. Use of renewable resources to make the sport products.

. Implementation of common high standards for the wellbeing of all employees.

. use suppliers who are socially responsible.

. Implementation of long term socially responsible aim rather than short term profit objectives.

. Willingness to pay cost of environmental protection.

. Establishment and implementation of ethical codes of practice to become a socially responsible organization.

Q4 Evaluate the advantages and disadvantages to Nike, Inc. of aiming to be a socially

responsibility organization.

Nike, Inc needs to be a socially responsibility organization to concern its stakeholders of consumers,

employees, environment benefit. Nike, Inc was a organization to become more increasing global,

it is becoming more difficult to ensure ethical to supply chain and takes on ethical approach to

managing the workplace that extends beyond organizational national and cultural boundaries.

For example, Nike, Inc. has strong research and development apartments is because Nike's sport products are

manufactured in low wage factories in the far East countries. Therefore they can concentrate on

marketing image and research project. However, it's low salary workers need have human right
protection to rise their reasonable wage level. Thus it is not a socially responsibility organization, it
needs to implement a socially responsibility organization to make stakeholders to believe in the future.
However, it will have advantages and disadvantages during it plan to achieve a social responsibility
organization.

On advantages hand, it can promote good public image, it is pride of employees can be a motivator,
it is being ahead of changes in law which can give time to find cheaper solution and it can avoid
costly bad media publicity on damaging natural environment issues.

On the disadvantages hand, it needs to increase cost to produce new sport products, it needs to take
manpower and attention from other important aims and objectives, it's result will be long teem rather than
short term, stakeholders will be conflict on socially responsible and ethical issues and it is possible that
it will drop in profit due to increase costs and may have negative effect on share prices.

IV

The difference between internal and external stakeholders

Q1 Using examples from the case study, explain the differences between internal and external
stakeholders.

Stakeholders are groups of people or individual who can be affected or is affected to gain advantages or
disadvantages by the achievement of purpose and action taken by an organization. Stakeholders can be
individuals, communities, social groups organizations. For example, stakeholders in a forest policy might
include people who live in or near the relevant forests, people who live further away who live further
away who use those forests, settlers from where in the country or abroad.

British GCM Co does mining/coal project scheme in Bangladesh country.

It's internal stakeholders are people who own or work for it's mining/coal project in Bangladesh country. For

example, shareholders, managers, workers, directors etc all staffs.

It's external stakeholders are people who do not work for or own a business for it's mining/coal

project scheme in Bangladesh country. For example, Bangladesh country Government, the world development

movement organization, the Asian development bank loan lender, local residents, international campaign

groups, local newspapers and TV channels, local farmers and landowners etc.

Q2 Explain the benefits of any two stakeholder groups resulting from this mine project.

Stakeholders group have benefits from GCM Co mine project scheme in Bangladesh country which

include GCM employees, GCM shareholders, landowners, Asian development bank, suppliers etc.

GCM Co needs invest large expansion of its coal/mining business project by building a new head office

and coal/mine site to develop natural resource in Bangladesh country.

Possible benefits impact on Bangladesh country central and/or local Government which larger new

head office will lead to increase payments to Bangladesh country local Government through local business

taxation , a mining project would provide a boost to the Bangladesh country economy, a lot of tonnes of coal
would be exported, it brings a valuable foreign currency for the economy. The mine/coal could also supply
cheap coal for power generation in Bangladesh country providing a cheap source of electricity and further
boosting the economy. Jobs would also be created, helping the Government to achieve its macro economies
objectives as well as local community, the mine project would employment and a some of income to members
of the local population. This income will be spent on local services and goods, further benefiting the local
community.
Possible benefits impact on Bangladesh country suppliers of information technology to provide service to
GCM Co to help them to earn more income because it needs new information technology coal/mine productive
machines to rise coal workers efficiency and shorten time to produce coal production. It may lead to reduce
mining/coal nature waste to produce more coal/mining natural resource from information technological
machines. Thus, it can raise to sell more coal/mining numbers from high information technological machines
to earn more profit to shareholders.
Q3 Explain the disadvantages to any two stakeholder groups resulting from this mine project.
The mine/coal project needs much lands physically and economically displace many people. This
displacement will take place in one of the most densely populated countries in the world and will
destroy a critical agricultural region in the Bangladesh country.

It will cause disadvantages to local community, the environmental damage is caused by mining, it
would be indicated by land development movement. The mining would spoil landscape and cause
diversion of a river and destruction of a forest, will resulting impact on those who depend on the
forest for making living. For example, farmers and local community homes would have to be
relocated.

It will cause disadvantages to it's employees, the mining/ coal project may being employees into conflict
with the local community and who are against the mine/coal job. Although workers need the work, who
may feel uncomfortable about the significant destruction of environment being caused by the mining/ coal
project.

Q4 Discuss the ways in which GCM could reduce the impact of the disadvantages it has
created for stakeholder groups negatively affected by the mine.
GCM co can reduce impact of disadvantages , it has created for stakeholder groups negatively affected
by mining/coal project scheme in Bangladesh country.
They include that workers whose homes are moved, so GCM Co can offer compensation and it can build better
home for them, landowners who have land forcibly purchased, so GCM Co can offer more than the current
market price and arrange meetings to explain that they will be compensated, farmers whose land now has no

water due to relocated river, so GCM Co can offer compensation and/or jobs in the new mining/coal to family members.

• 24 •

V

Limited company strategies

Q1 Explain the following terms from the text:

1a Public limited company

Public limited company means an incorporated limited liability business whose shares are traded

publicly on the stock exchange and whose reports and accounts are publicly available.

1b Multinational retailer

This is a chain of shops that operates in various countries in addition to the country in which its

headquarters is located.

1c Technological advances

These are innovations in machinery, equipment or computer systems which may allow the

business to improve efficiency of operation and /or economies of scale.

Q2 Explain how rapid economic growth in China might

impact on one aspect of Carrefour's business
strategy.

Business planning is a management-directed process of identifying long-term goals for a business or
business segment, and formulating realistic strategies for reaching those goals. Through planning,
HYPERLINK   "http://www.referenceforbusiness.com/encyclopedia/Kor-Man/Management.html"   management decides what objectives to pursue during a future period, and what actions to undertake
to achieve those objectives.

Carrefour was the world's first department store opened in Paris, France in 1959. Although it didn't
enter China market unteil 1995, the speed of its development in China has been faster than any other
countried. To June of 2006, Carrefour had established 78 chain stores in China, starting with
first store in Beijing, Carrefour arrived in Shanghai and Shenzhen in 1996.

Carrefour developed so rapidly in China because China can offer it very good economic benefit
and development of Carrefour in China has realized economies of scale. Thus, Carrefour one aspect of
business strategy is to such as the establishment of distribution centres to reduce transport and
distribution costs to expand more supermarket in China different cities.

For example, Carrefour's supermarkets have established special counters for quality line foods.

They havea clear brand logo, foods are packaged, not only quality line label, but also with supplier
information on a traceable barcode. The quality line is control and supervision by Carrefour raw
and freash agribulture food throughout the supply chain from planting and processing to distribution,
in order to guarantee the quality and safety of foods of Carrefour own brand.

The quality line has a number a key aims to maintain traceability throughout the supply chain from
planting to eating, to produce agriculture food with no pesticide reside, to ensure quality is consistent
and reliable, to use environment friendly production and processing technologoes and produce
at a price acceptable to market to be lower than truly organic food because only a few consumers can
afford organiz food.

It decentralized management. It divided its Chinese to structure into four regions of East China,
South China, North China and middle China. It used local partners, such as Shanghainese partner
in Shanghai, a Cantonese partner in Guangzhou and a Beijing partner in Beijing.
It also employed China storemanagers to manage it's supermarkets, their duties include foods on
orders, purchasing, pricing supplier selection, arrangement and store displays, employees
recruitment and negotiating promotional campaigns etc. Employing foreign Chineses to manage

its supermarkets in China is more acceptable to it local clients in China.

Moreover, Carrefour has a variety of cooperative ways of working with agriculture food
suppliers in China by joint operation. Thus, Carrefour business strategy competes against its
supermarket competitors on the basic of price, convenience and customer experience.
In conclusion, this business strategy is such as the establishment of distribution centres in China, it
achieved Carrefour could expanded established 78 chain stores in China in 2006.

Q3 Analyze the social changes that may be taking place in China which could influence Carrefour's
activities in China.
Since the mid-1990 year, changes have taken place in consumers' demands for agriculture food in
China, citizen's incomes have increased rapidly, rapid growth of Gross domestic product per capita.
People's food demands have changed from quantity to quality, safety and diversity, rise in education levels
and improvement in social welfare and improved communication with other countries.

The first supermarkets were developed rapidly in China from 1990 and China's entry into the world
trading to begin to open its retail market in general and in 2004 foreign businesses entered China's market and
the increasing competition among and between supermarkets and traditional retail stores.

China consumers traditionally buy raw and fresh agriculture food every day. So the quality and availability
of raw and fresh agriculture food has become an important measurement of supermarkets' attractiveness
to clients. Many supermarkets provide organic and green agriculture foods in their stores too (Hu, D. 2005).
Because China economic growth to cause social changes, it could influence Carrefour
carried on these activities sell its agriculture foods in its China supermarkets as below:

Although economic development and improvement in people's living standards, China customers demand
the quality of raw and fresh agriculture food and choice of varieties and safety agriculture food in China
are rising. Thus, Carrefour classifies these raw and fresh agriculture food into five categories: Fish, meat,
fruit and vegetables, salads and breads. Carrefour must keep these foods to save in clean and cold store room
to keep all foods to be fresh to prepare to sell to it's clients from Fresh transportation process.

China social changes cause it has many diverse cultures and consumers. For example, Beijing drink beer
social changes adapt to local tastes and preferences in these areas. Carrefour introduces new products, such
as wine to China and promotes wine fairs and educates Chinese how to drink wine and what foods
it goes with. Carrefour imports wine to Chinese to adapt to local taste or by using its knowledge from Taiwan.

Carrefour's selling strategies also be changed to adapt to sell

fish alive and sell frozen fish to the China bigger
cities preferred to buy fish alive, right out of fish tanks.
Chinese west and middle China preferred to purchase
frozen fish because they are further away from the coast
and want fish to be fresh. Thus China social changes
also change Carrefour's fish sale behaviour in China
supermarkets to adapt to local consumer and shopping
behaviours.

Rising Asian middle class and China consumers are more
conscience of health and environment and Carrefour
can have its own line of organic foods and it stocks fair
trade products and it has also reduced energy
energy consumption and disposable plastic bag
numbers in China is a opportunity to Carrefour to do food
sale
business.

In conclusion, China social changes brought Chinese
consumers like to compare different brands. Thus,
Carrefour must introduce larger shelves in order to
place all different brands in one areas in supermarkets.

Reference
Hu, Dinghuan (2005), On the binary structure of
agriculture food: The impact of supermarket development
on the agriculture sector and agriculture food safety,
Chinese Rural Economy, no.2 pp.12-17.
Q4 Produce a PEST analysis for Carrefour as it plans to
open new stores in Western China.
PEST analysis elements include political, economic,
social and technological aspects.

As Carrefour plans to open new stores in Western China. It needs to produce a PEST analysis to help it
to know China external environments factors to affect it's business objective and strategies to achieve
its business aim in China supermarket market successfully.

On the political aspect, China opens world trading market to let different countries investors to establish
their businesses in Western China. This Carrefour can enter China supermarket market more easily.

On the economic aspect, the current devaluation of the Euro will import more expensive to European
businesses. This is a threat to Carrefour to enter western market, Rising Asian middle class in
Western China can increase supermarket food purchase demand.

On the social aspect, Western China consumers are more conscience of health and environment and Carrefour
can have its own line of organic foods and it stocks fair trade products and it has also reduced energy
energy consumption and disposable plastic bag numbers in Western China. It is a opportunity to Carrefour to do
supermarket business in Western China.

On the technological aspect, social networking sites provide an opportunity for Carrefour supermarket
because which can be used to increase customer loyalty to brand, e.g. twitter and face book can be used to

create commonly for loyal of Carrefour's clients in Western China easily.

VI

SWOT analysis

Q1 Produce a SWOT analysis for Four Season Leisure's current position.

A SWOT analysis is a form of strategic analysis that identifies and analyses the internal strengths and

weaknesses and external opportunities and threats that will influence the future direction and success of a

business. Thus, a SWOT analysis provides information that can be helpful in matching the firm's resources

and strengths to the competitive environment in which it operates. It is useful in strategy formation and

selection.

Four Season Leisure's SWOT analysis for current position as below:

Internal strengths: Thirty years of providing holidays to high income European and North American

consumers travel business experiences to build most famous brands in the Caribbean, it has attributed

the group's relative success to effective management from a team of people that have considerable knowledge and expertise in the travel market.

Internal Weaknesses: It's concentration in the Caribbean travel market is weakness.

External opportunities: The world economic slow down and it causes traveller demands decrease,

expanding into some of the new destinations that its customers are interested in visiting.

External threats: Increasing Four Season Leisure's share of the travel market, all inclusive holiday resort

market, The competition is from new holiday destination such as Dubai.

Q2a Construct a fully labelled decision tree showing Four Season's options.

Four Season's decision tree

economic conditions initial cost projected profit
expected value
Option 1: Open new resort ($120 million) fast growth $40 million x20%
in Dubai

normal growth $200 million x 50%

recession -($100 million x 30%)

Option 2: Open new resort
in Thailand ($150 million) fast growth $500 million x 20%

normal growth $300 million x 50%

recession -($50 million x 30%)

Option 3: Upgrade existing ($80 million) fast growth $150 million x 20%
existing resorts

in Caribbean normal growth $120 million x 50%
recession -(%100 million x 30%)

Q2b Calculate the expected values for each option.
Four Season leisure expected values as below:
Option 1
fast growth $40 million x20% + normal growth $200 million x 50% - recession ($100 million x 30%)
Thus option 1 expected value is $78 million

Option 2
fast growth $500 million x 20% + normal growth $300 million x 50% - recession ($50 million x 30%)
Thus option 2 expected value is $235 million

Option 3
fast growth $150 million x 20% + normal growth $120 million x 50% - recession ($100 million x 30%)
Thus option 3 expected value is $ 60 million
Q2c On financial grounds state which option Four Seasons should choose.
Four Season Leisure will choose option 2 because it's expected value is $ 235 million and it's
economic condition initial cost is $150 million, it can earn predict profit is $85 million.
However, the other two options is both initial cost amount is much than expected value
, so it have predicted loss.

Q2d Analyse one weakness for Four Seasons of using decision trees as a basis for making
this business decision.

Decision trees is a technique that considers the value of the options available and the chance

of them occurring. It is a diagram that sets out the options connected with a decision and the

outcomes and economic returns that may result.

Four Season leisure uses decision trees to make business decision to predict which travel

destination option can earn the largest expect value, if it evaluates the fast growth,

normal growth and recession occurrence chance is wrong, it will choose the expect value

is not the nest financial return. Thus decision trees has possible the incorrect fast growth,

normal growth and recession to predict for these travel destination expect value.

VII

Internal and external growth

Q1 Use the case study to explain the difference between internal and external growth.

Traffic clothing plc produces suits and dresses and sells them to major retailers in several

countries. It plan to grow it's clothing manufacturing business to overseas.

Internal growth can be achieved in a number of ways and these forms of growth can lead

to differing effects on stakeholder groups, such as customers, workers and competitors.

Reasons include to plan these internal growth strategy of sale turnover have grown

by around 15% each year, but a slower rate than some competitors, aims to increase

much profit. For example, Traffic clothing plc plans to open own clothing retailer

shops in towns and cities to offer customers a top quality shopping experience to allow
suits and dresses differentiation in a crowded markets , aims to increase market
share in clothing industry. Increased economic of scale of internal growth strategy,
traffic low prices have been possible due to the opening of low cost factories in
developing countries.

External growth means business expansion is achieved by means of merging with or
taking over another business from either the same or a different industry.
It's external growth strategy could be achieved by aggressive takeover either other
clothing producers or material suppliers to achieve cost leadership, it would focused on a
small, higher in come market segment in several overseas markets.
This could be reinforced with a merger with a prestige clothing retailer.

Q2 Explain how the business increased sales revenue, yet gained no increase in profits for the
last three years.
Traffic clothing plc can increased sale revenue by around 15% each year, yet gained to increase in
profits for the last three years.
The reasons include these factors, new competitors were entering the clothing market and driving down
prices, raw material prices for both natural and man-made inputs were rising, the number of merger between

large clothing retailers had increased that bargaining power when dealing with producers like Traffic.

Q3 Assess the likely advantages and disadvantages of a cost leadership strategy for this business.

The advantages and disadvantages of a cost leadership strategy for Traffic clothing plc manufacturing

business as below:

Cost leadership strategy means the lowest cost producer in the industry for a certain level of product

quality will allow the firm to make higher profits than competitors or if the businessman lowers its

prices below the average of competitors, to increase market share. This strategy usually targets a broad

rather than a niche market, e.g. Ryanair, one of Europe's largest and most profitable airlines, is also

the lowest average cost airline. Thus, traffic clothing plc adapts this cost leadership strategy either producers

suits and dresses due to opening of low cost factories in developing countries to sell to major retailers in

several countries at average industry prices to earn higher profit than clothing competitors or below

industry average prices to gain market share.

The cost leadership advantages to Traffic clothing plc include that it can spend more extra money to invest

to buy of high level of advanced clothing production machines to shorten time of the clothing manufacturing

process in efficient production methods for rise to produce many suits and dresses numbers to sell to major

retailers in several countries, economic of scale to produce suits and dresses to reduce clothing manufacturing cost for long time.

However, cost leadership strategy also has these disadvantages to Traffic clothing plc includes that it could be
achieved b aggressive takeover of either other clothing producers or material suppliers to achieve cost
leadership if it expanded its clothing manufacturing business by means of merging to them to taking one
another business from either the clothing manufacturing industry or clothing retail industry.
Thus, it would give cost leadership benefits to it's competitors in clothing manufacturers or
clothing retailers.

Q4 Assess the likely advantages and disadvantages of a differentiation or a focused strategy for
this business.
The advantages and disadvantages of a differentiation or a focused strategy for Traffic clothing plc as below:
Differentiation strategy advantages involves developing a product or service that offers unique features valued
clients.
Traffic clothing plc can own clothing retail shops in itself and several countries to offer customers a
top quality shopping experience, this will allow differentiation in a crowed market.
Traffic clothing plc can rise suits and dresses sale value added to its clothing product or provide training
to raise sale people service performance by these features may allow it to charge a premium price for it
when it's clients feel a top quality shopping experience from its sale people service performance. It can

help strong sales team able to promote the perceived strengths of its brand and its suits and dresses clothing

products, rising Traffic clothing plc corporate reputation for innovation and quality and it can have extra

money to prepare excellent research and development clothing manufacturing machine facilities.

However, differentiation strategy has disadvantages to it, it needs spend much money to invest

to buy high speed and advanced clothing manufacturing technological machines to help it to rise to

produce high quality and unique of suits and dresses clothing products in the short time and it needs

to lend loan from banks if it has no enough capital to buy these clothing manufacturing machines.

The focused strategy concentrates on a narrow market segment, aiming to achieve either a cost

advantages or differentiation. This can lead to a high degree of customer loyalty within the market

segment.

Traffic clothing plc focused strategy could be achieved by aggressive takeovers of either other

clothing producers or material suppliers to achieve cost leadership, focusing on a smaller, higher

income market segment. This could be reinforced with a merger with a prestige clothing

retailer.

Advantages include Traffic clothing plc can concentrate on sell its suits and dresses clothing

products to several countries, eg. young age between 20 to 40 male or female group clients.

However, disadvantages include, it needs to time to gather information about it's client age target to choose
which major several countries and the young age group in different countries of clients .

If it's clothing sale numbers reduced, even it will have too many old clothing stocks to keep in its warehouse,
it has no power to sell these old clothing stocks for long time.

These old clothing stocks would be obsolete, it's clients won't willing to accept to buy old style clothing or
damaged clothing in warehouse to keep long time.

VIII

Change Management

Q1 define the term change management

Change management involves planning, implementing, controlling, and reviewing the movement

of an organization from its current state to a new one.

The change management includes external and internal factors. Planned change results from deliberate

decisions to alter an organization and unplanned change is imposed on the organization and is often

unforeseen.

Internal forces for change include things like declining effectiveness (resignations or major accidents),

changes in employee expectations and changes in the work climate, e.g. organizations need to develop

and improve reasons.

External forces for change include globalization, workforce diversity, technological innovation, ethics. Change may take one of three forms, incremental change is relatively small in scope and as such,

results in small improvements. Strategic change is a larger scale approach that is similar to a restructuring

effort.

Thus, change management moves the organization forward a different and sometimes, unknown future state.

Q2 Explain the role a project term might have in changing the direction of HMV.

Change management is a complex and large subject area which tends to form part of higher level questions.

Project team means a group of employees entrusted with managing a defined project (this may be a change

management project). The team may consist of special employees required from the success of the

new project.

Thus HMV music entertainment business project team role and responsibilities may include:

Identification of areas of change, e.g. changing by acquisition, pure MHV loyalty card scheme, 50%

stake in 7 digital, pilot HMV (Urzon -branded cinema in Wimbledon), establishment of new vision

and objectivity to design new organization management structure to adapt new management structure

after HMV music entertainment business takeovers HAMA Group, ensuring resources are enough to used

in planning change, e.g. timing, legal, marketing development etc requiring, implementing and controlling

and reviewing if planning process and reducing conflict avoidance measures and education of major

shareholders. e.g. HMV music entertainment business major shareholders who must need to approve the

MAMA music entertainment Group major shareholders offer during their communication must be needed to
involve in their every time board of meeting in decision making process, project team needs to support staffs,
giving negotiation, reducing threatening where there is still restrain to them.

Q3 Analyze two driving forces and two restraining forces which are influencing HMV's
transformation plan as it tries to change the direction of the organization.

Driving forces which are influencing it (HMV company) tries to change the direction of organization
successfully include: falling sales and growth of illegal download is existing in music entertainment market,
which may make internal stakeholders more willing to co-operate, as well as management enthusiasm is for
expanding into live music as a new marker. These is external and internal factors support to achieve takeover
planning is successfully.

Restraining forces which are influencing it (HMV company) tries to takeover MAMA Group to change
direction of organization successfully. HMV company may not be recognized as player in the live music market
because it lacks management expertise in the cinema market and artist areas and MAMA Group which is focus
on these market areas, instead of music area; HMV's takeover offer for MAMA Group is subject to
approval from shareholders, who are concerned about HMV moving into a market where it has limited direct

experience, along with prospects of raising finance to fund the takeover. This contrasts with the enthusiastic

view of HMV's management who are keen to explore the prospects of live music as a new market. These are

external and internal factors threat to implement takeover planning successfully.

Q4 Using an appropriate businesses model, analyse how HMV's proposed takeover of the

MAMA Group will give it a competitive advantage in the music industry.

Entertainment music firm HMV is expanding its presence in the live music market by buying venue owner

MAMA Group for $46 million. MAMA group runs concert venues including the Hammersmith Apollo in

London. MAMA Group also owns other interests, e.g. an artist management business representing,

artic monkeys etc vaccines business areas.

A force field business model should be constructed with driving and restraining forces identified on

opposing sides in columns to the left and right of a centrally recognised proposal for HMV Group change

to takeover of HAMA Group in music industry.

Each force should have on estimated score noted beside it (1 is the most weak to 5 is the most strong) and these

should be totalled at the bottom of each column. Thus, the questionnaires can analyze how HMV proposed

takeover of MAMA Group will give it a competitive advantage in music market.

HMV music entertainment company needs for a new area of operation to compensate for problems in

traditional areas in music industry.

The Driving forces factors estimated score is needed for change include that it needs enthusiasm of

management, wider market (spreads operational risk), improving profitability aim every year, accessing

to new expertise in MAMA group etc factors.

The restraining forces against factors estimated score for change is who the shareholders need spend

too much cost to approve the takeover include that HMV and MAMA Groups are two different music

company. They have differences in corporate cultures need to adapt if HAMA Group wanted takeover

MAMA Group to operate its business successfully, HMA Group needs much time and training to takeover

MAMA Group, it is possible that there is potential staff redundancies change occurrence etc factors.

These are HMV Group external and internal factors to analyse how HMV's proposed takeover of the

MAMA Group will give it a competitive advantage in the music industry.

IX
Globalization

Q1 Define the term globalisation

Globalization means integration of world economies through free trade, free flow of capital and cheaper

foreign labour markets. The free trade of goods, capital ad labour in worldwide markets. It is

unrestricted by trade barriers, such as tariffs.

On the global stage, competitive advantages are gained by creating, transferring and exploiting competences across operations and locations internationally.

Economic effects of globalization include global economic growth and distribution.

Globalization results multinational organizations are heavily involved in global changes. Many of these organizations are pursuing joint ventures with firms from other countries.

Q2 Explain two potential advantages to Kraft of taking over Cadbury

Takeover means one business, usually larger one, buys controlling interest of another business.

Kraft is USA one chocolate and cheese and cake foods sale company, it takes over Cadbury UK chocolate

company potential advantages include that instant growth to enter European chocolate market in short term;

increasing geographic and chocolate markets expanding to European market spread; acquired European

chocolate manufacturing local experts skills and European supply chain contacts to suppliers more easier;

acquisition may be at lower than the chocolate market value of the assets if the acquired business is in

difficulty.

Q3 Analyze the problems Kraft might experience as it tries to enter the European chocolate

market.

Kraft is one USA chocolate, cheese and cake foods sale company, it tries to enter the European chocolate

market, it might experience these problems.

It can lack to understand of European local culture to known European clients chocolate taste, it can lack

ability to contract and supply a distribution chains to enter European chocolate easily, A lot of

European who don't accept to eat America brand chocolate, cheese and cake foods easily,

Kraft's American staffs will feel difficult to speak European language to work in European, Kraft's

American staffs need to adapt time difference to work in European, different European consumer law

regards chocolate, cheese and cake foods product content, spending advertising to attract European

consumers.

Q4 Discuss how Ansoff's matrix model might have been

useful to Kraft in making the decision
to take over Cadbury.

Ansoff's matrix can make the decision to help Kraft to take over Cadbury in chocolate market.

It can help it's business to analyze how to expand market growth and product growth strategies, it

provides a formal basis for logical and systematic analysis to that all options are considered and

Kraft can encourage consideration of alternative strategic options.

Kraft might have these business strategies in making the decision to take over Cadbury.

Market penetration strategy means existing products in existing markets. Although, this strategy has no

applicable to Kraft because Kraft has no it's USA brand chocolates to exist presence in the European chocolate
market.

However, after it takes over Cadbury in European chocolate market successfully, it can increase it Kraft

chocolate numbers to European largely. It is low risk strategy, may be achieved by improving Kraft and

Cadbury chocolate product element mix, promotion can be forced on future European existing clients to
make more purchase.

Market development strategy means existing products enter to new markets. Kraft may see opportunity

to reposition some existing European Cadbury brands chocolate foods to sell to new chocolate market.

For example: Asian countries include Hong Kong, Taiwan, China, Japan etc. It is medium risk strategy,

it can be risky if have little knowledge of the new market, Kraft needs new distribution channels to sell
these Asian countries new chocolate markets.

Product development strategy means new products enter new markets. Kraft and Cadbury brand chocolates
may to renew to resign their package design and may give discount to pricing to be adapted to these Asian
countries new chocolate market. It is medium risk strategy, it may be suitable if Kraft and Cadbury chocolate
food products have reached saturation or decline. It is a reason why Kraft acquires Cadbury chocolate business.
Diversification means new products enter in new markets. It is high risk strategy, it can gain market share in
existing markets, it is spread risk and it is often a reason why businesses acquire new businesses.
For example, Kraft and Cadbury co-operate to produce new taste of chocolates, cheeses and cake foods to
sell to Asia countries, e.g. China, Hong Kong , Japan, Korean etc countries.

X

human resource management

Q1a. Explain human resource management

This is the strategic approach to the effective management of an organization's workers,
so that who help the business gain a competitive advantage.

Q1b. Explain recruitment

This is the process of identifying the need for a new employee, defining the job to be
filled and the types of staff needed to fill it, attracting suitable candidates for the job and
selecting the best one.

Q1c. Explain part time/temporary contract

A contract is a legal document that sets out the terms and conditions governing an employee's job.

For a temporary contract this is valid for a fixed time period, e.g. six months or one year working

period. For a part time job, this is for less than the normal full working week, e.g. 25 hours out of

a possible 40 full time hours per week.

The hourly paid academic contract is a means of permitting flexibility in managing the delivery

of the academic programme. It allows the college to broaden the scope of teaching by including

specialist contributions and more usually, it provides a way of dealing with contingencies, such as

unexpected absence or unplanned but temporary increases in workload.

Q2 Explain benefits to college of workplace planning

Workplace planning means this is the establishment of the staff number and skills of the workplace required by

the business (college) to meet future objectives. Benefits of workplace planning to college school college

management think and plan ahead so that there is time to make major read to strategy if human resources

function can't support it.

Efforts to find school staffs, e.g. lecturers, college office administration positions etc. which need select either

from outside advertisement or inside staff promotion methods is more suitable for someone is difficult to fill

college any positions can be started well in advance.

College can advance to prepare which positions are necessary training, which can be identified and found what
are necessary training to get skills to work for identified positions.

During the college decides and exact workforce number for every department is needed, it will not reduce any
college staffs. For example, science and geography subject departments won't reduce any lecturers next year
if college has working planning to predict how many lecturers are needed in these two subject departments.
Thus, college can take advantage of natural wastage rather than making redundancies which can be costly and
de-motivating and it is bad for college reputation if it often dismiss any staffs suddenly.

What is appropriate for an organization to use depends on how easily it can be implemented and the ease
can be implemented and the ease with which it can be tailored to the situation?

Thus, working planning is long term and takes plan in the context of many other internal and external
influences, so it is not easy to say whether or not it work.

In conclusion, the benefits of conducting workforce planning are that it helps college to get the right people in
the right job of the right time. It allows for a more effective and efficient use of workers and for organizing
to prepare for restructuring, reducing or expanding their reducing or expanding their workforces. In additions,

the process of workforce planning aids organizations by providing objectives which integrate the various units
and allow employees space and time to think about common goals for the future.
Q3 Analyze arguments against offering full time and permanent employment contracts to
the new office staff and lecturers

Full time and permanent employment means a contract is a legal document that sets out the terms and
conditions governing an employee's job. For a full time and permanent contract, this is valid for permanent
period, but it has probationary period to test the employee whether who has skill and knowledge to do the
job. For example, three months or one month probationary period and the normal full working week is a
possible 30 hours at least.

Arguments against offering full time and permanent employment contracts to the new office staff and
lecturers for college employer. It can be costly to make a permanent full time employee redundant if the
business (college) doesn't need them any more and it can not allow greater for changing market flexibility
conditions, e.g. the enrolling student numbers are suddenly falling in this year.
Select college will need three more administration workers and ten more lecturers. Offering part time
and temporary contracts to three office workers which won't need to provide long service pension and
full time salaries and insurance etc benefits to them, it can save more expenditure in long term.

However, Select college needs to employ ten more lectures to teach it's science and geography

students. Offering full time and permanent employment contracts is more right than offering

full time and temporary employment contracts or part time and temporary employment contracts

to these ten lecturers because who will not have more motivation to keep good staff to Select college

if who know to work temporarily as well as who will feel unfair if who know the old lecturers

are working full time employment contract.

Hence, I recommend that Select college can offer part time or temporary variable hour employment contracts to

these three new office staff and it also need minimum guaranteed income to give to college new office staff.

Otherwise, it needs to offer full time and permanent employment contracts to these ten lecturers because it's

geography and science subject students will increase possibly, so who needs these ten lecturers to teach them

for long term.

Q4 Evaluate the best ways for college to select the lecturers.

Recruitment is the process of identifying the need for a new employee, defining the job to be filled and the type

of staff needed to fill it, attracting suitable candidates for the job and selecting the best one.

As this college needs to select who is the right applicant when it has new lecturers vacancy. It needs to

evaluate which are the best ways to select applicant to fill this lecture positions. I shall recommend that the best ways to this college to select and this recruit the new lecturer applicants.

The best ways to recruit and select the new lecturer applicants for this college include:
The first way is the employing specialist recruitment agency to help it to carry on selecting and recruiting
process. It begins to advertise lecturer vacancies, interviewing the applicants who apply these lecturer
positions till to selecting applicants who own the teaching skill and knowledge to fill any subject teaching
vacancies for these lecturer positions.

The reason is because lecturers need have high educated knowledge and work experience, any specialist
recruitment agency is the educational professionals to help this college to find the right applicants to do the
lecturer positions. Thus this college can employ lecturers from specialist recruitment agency employment
service in the short time and this college doesn't need arrange any subject lecturers who need to spend
too much time to carrying on interviewing to select the best lecturers.

Another way is college can employ a recruitment agency who identifies candidates, then the college interviews
them and makes the final decision.

Next way is college internet employment method, applicants can enter college website to download their
resumes to let this college human resource department to read to select who can be interviewed before the due
date.

The final way is the college can do all employment advertisement, interview and select the right applicants to

do the right lecturer positions to teach the different subjects by all themselves.

However, I shall recommend that specialist recruitment agency employment is the best way to select lecturers.

College reward framework is based on the principle of equal pay for work of equal value and aims to be

flexible and variable enough to ensure that the college is competitive and able to recruit, support and retain

high quality specialist staff to achieve college objectives in terms of learning and teaching, scholarship and

research, and knowledge exchange. Thus, specialist recruitment agency employment shall be an efficient

and effective recruitment and selection method to develop in negotiation with college senior managers and

college recruitment department.

XI
Delaying

Q1 a. Explaining delaying

Delaying means that large organizations flatten their hierarchies. Flattening or delaying, as it is also known

typically elimination of layers in a firm's organizational hierarchy and the broadening of manager's spans

of control.

Q1 b. Explaining cultural conflict

Cultural conflict (differences) also exist in the organizational workplace and impact on human resource

management. When one organization's any department exists different countries staffs who work together,

large organization will have more cultural conflict occurrence between different countries staffs shall

have different personal ideas, education background and working experience and experience to cause

more cultural difference in large organizational departments. Otherwise, small organizations will exist less cultural conflict because small number of different countries staffs are needed.

Q2 Why cultural conflict seems to exist in Mitsubishi Motors (MMC) Ltd, Japan car maker?

Mitsubishi Motors Ltd reorganises structural Mitsubishi Motors (MMC), the Japanese car maker,
it is 37% owned by Daimler Chrysler, revealed significant changes to its senior and middle management
structure at a shareholders' meeting. The changes reflected between the company's incoming German
managers and established executives who found it difficult adjusting to the new culture.
The restructuring aimed to let some old managers to adapt new management change and other some
old managers were to be offered early retirement.

Victoria Emerson, president announced 60 senior staff advisers who were of an advance age and
made a marginal contribution to the company despite remuneration would be removed.
Then, she was made chief operation officer appointed a 100 team comprising about 25 mainly
non Japanese executives. This team is drawn from different departments, was responsible for
overseeing the implementation of the company's restructuring plan.

Some long term service members of Mitsubishi Motors (MMC) Ltd 's middle and upper management
resented the presence and power of the company team, all of whom were under 40 years old and who

were controlling the strategic direction of it.

The tension between the 100 team (chief operation officer team) and some of MMC 's managers was
described as Japanese managers with a job for life attitude. This is not part of German management
culture. Thus it will have cultural conflict in possible.

Mitsubishi Motors (Ltd) organizational change emphasizes changes in patterns of behaviour, values,
meanings. Thus organizational culture will also change to Mitsubishi culture is often defined as that
which is shared by and/or unique to a given organization or group, the social holds together a
potentially diverse group organizational members.

Various levels and divisions of Mitsubishi Motors Ltd with have different culture conflict of its
organizational hierarchy share a similar viewpoint.

For example, Mitsubishi Motors ltd top executive's commitment is to the value of confronting conflicts
and then cited evidence from fiercely argumentative group decision making meetings to demonstrate
that Mitsubishi Motors Ltd leaders' values were shared and enacted by power level employees.
Thus, Mitsubishi Motors Ltd cultural change is needed some different countries' staffs will change their
culture to adopt any different countries' staffs culture to work together in Mitsubishi staffs culture to work
together in Mitsubishi Motors Ltd organizations' strategic, business and operative hierarchy levels.

In summary, culture conflict occurs in Mitsubishi Motors Ltd organization because the different countries
managers, staffs occupational, educational, working experience background are very different before
who choose to work in this company.
Q3 Analyze possible benefits to MMC of reducing the chain of command through delaying.

Benefits of flattening flow primarily from pushing decisions downward to enhance customer and market
responsiveness and to improve accountability and morale. Has flattening delivered on its promise to push
decisions downward?

Whether Mitsubishi Motors Ltd have delayer and flattened organizational structure can exhibit were control
and decision making at the top. The conventional view of flattening, I find that Mitsubishi Motors Ltd CEO
eliminated layers in the management ranks, broadened their spans of control and changed pay structures in
ways.

CEO and other members of senior management who make resource allocation decisions that ultimately
determine Mitsubishi Motors Ltd strategy and performance . Flattening transferred some decision managers
to functional managers at the top and flattening is associated with increased CEO involvement with direct
reports and the second level of top management .

Corporate structure is as a form of internal governance.

Shape how decisions are made and how information is
communicated and processed. Another essential element of corporate structure is the compensation scheme that
align managerial incentives and guide decision making.

Mitsubishi Motors Ltd hierarchies have changed dramatically. CEO have flattened the hierarchical structure of
senior management: they delayer and eliminated management levels and broadened their span of control. Many
CEO eliminated the chief operating officer position and increased the number of division managers reporting
directly to the CEO. The same CEO also broadened span of control significantly and increase the number of
functional managers (e.g. CFO etc) reporting directly to them.
Q4 Discuss possible consequences for efficiency of business of new management structure in Mitsubishi
Motors (MML), Japan car maker.

Firms dramatically changes the structure of management compensation by increasing emphasis on performance
pay (bonuses, stock options) which is relative to base salaries.

Mitsubishi Motors Ltd is from a multidivisional Japan car maker change to a flattened organization structure
firm, increased span structure of control. Multidivisional structure is too much layers and more positions to
influence organizational communication.

Mitsubishi motors Ltd has systematically eliminated layers in the hierarchical structure of senior management.

Part of this delayer can be attributed to the elimination of key senior management positions.

Thus, possible consequences for efficiency of business of new management structure in Mitsubishi

Motors (MML), Japan car maker which include benefits to CEO who has more direct connections deeper in

organizations and is potentially more involved in decision making across more organizational units. Thus,

division managers' decision making is subject to more direct oversight by CEO assigned who exercises more

control and pushes decisions up a form of centralization.

Another benefit, it can create organizational knowledge to solve crises which faces easily. For example, one to

uncertainty of the future, Japanese Mitsubishi Motors Ltd had to turn to resources outside the organization for

new knowledge and insight and the socio-cultural differences between Japan and the western world resulted in

their contrasting approaches to knowledge creation.

Tacit knowledge can't be communicated through manuals or theories. Instead , it is knowledge from Mitsubishi

Motors maker Ltd' s employees knowledge who gained through experience and knowledge linked to their

attitudes and beliefs. individual's ideas are highly value in Japanese Mitsubishi Motor maker Ltd and

suggestions and improvements are judged based on Mitsubishi Motor Ltd staffs' merits and is not by
the seniority or starting of the individuals in Mitsubishi Motor Ltd.

XII

Communication

Q1 Define the term effective communication

Effective communication is the exchange of information between people or groups with by written, oral, nonverbal organizational feedback.

Thus, effectiveness communication can help organizations to facility decision making and it can provides information by transmitting the data to identify and evaluate alternative choices, it can provide a release for emotional expression of feelings and is for fulfilment of employees, their work group exchange information with feedback need, it can motivate employees to know what is be done, how well who are doing and what can be done to improve performance.

Q2 Outline how this case could harm employer-employee relationships in this factory in the future.
Panasonic unified communication provides cost effective solutions for small, medium and large business

organizations. The solutions combine advanced business telephone products with business clients' user

productivity tools, networked directly to standard business application in office.

However, it's organization communicates bad news which can harm employer -employee relationships in

this factory in the future. The cause was the voice at the end of company telephone on 16 Oct. which

indicated there would be no redundancies among the 2400 strong work force at the Panasonic factory in

Cardiff. But two days later, there would be job cuts, limited to several hundred. On 22 Oct , 1300 people

were to be made redundant again. It's handling of the affair was bad management practice.

A manager of human resources is not the appropriate man to announce the bad news to let it's factory

workers to know the bad news. Hence, who had not already found another job at the time. It is not

fair to them.

Thus, this case could harm employer-employee relationships in this factory in the future as below:

It's employee shall lack of trust or management by their employer, it shall cause source of future

conflict again, Panasonic management staffs shall lack of respect to their employees for management

again, future belief of employee redundancy of rumours could create problems, worker insecurity

could result in loss of motivation, trends in low productivity and staff leaving shall increase.

All these factors could harm employer-employee relationships in this factory in the future and

in reality a combination of these factors could also harm future relationships between different

employees are likely to react in different ways. In fact, the factors could interact and have a

cause to effect result in all aspects of Panasonic company efficient and effective operation in the

future.

Q3 Evaluate the different ways in which Panasonic might communicate any future redundancies to staff

and the media. Refer to all aspects of effective communication, the appropriate sender and

receiver, the clarity of the message, the medium to be used and the opportunity for feedback.

Redundancies mean this is job loss due to employee's job no longer being required. This may be

because the business re-organizes or because it can no longer afford to employ the employee. Redundancy

may be compulsory or voluntary. For legal reasons redundancy needs to be formally stated in a letter,

whichever primary method of communication is used. However, I shall evaluate the different ways in

which Panasonic might communicate any future redundancies to staff and the media as below:

Suggestion one, group meetings:

Group meeting sender may be a senior UK executive and receivers is groups of workers, e.g. a

maximum of 30 worker numbers, the medium is speech and question and answer session, the opportunity
for feedback is possible but may be limited.

Meeting advantages include direct questions may be asked and followed up with more questions until full
understanding and satisfaction are achieved, the message may be reinforced with caring body language,
persuading verbal language speaking used may soften the message and/or be easier to understand. However,
meeting disadvantages also include questions may be limited to a few and workers shall lack brave enough to
ask questions in front of an audience, time limitation may mean that not all questions are asked, questions
thought of after the meeting may not be asked, some workers will have their meeting before others, this can
result in incorrect transmission of information and/or the feeling the some workers are considered more
important than others.

Suggestion two, One -one-one meetings:
One-on-one meeting sender may be senior department or human resource managers, many managers would be
needed to do this for mass redundancies and so the task would need to be split and receiver is each individual
worker, the medium is speech and opportunity for feedback is possible but may be limited.

One-on-one meeting advantages include direct questions may be asked and followed up with more questions
until full understanding and satisfaction are achieved, every employee can ask the questions which individually

concern them, the personal importance of each employee is recognised, the message may be reinforced with

caring body language, persuading language used may soften the message and/or be easier to understand.

One-on-one meeting disadvantages include the high stress, face to face situation may be for much for some

workers, questions thought of after the meeting may not be asked, some managers may conduct the meeting

better than others , special training may be needed in advance and this may cause rumours to spread, some

employees have had meeting, so rumours and stress will spread quickly, sequencing of meetings may be

different, come employees will have whose meeting before others, which may give the impression that

some employees are considered some important than others.

Suggestion three, letter:

Letter sender may be a senior UK executive who is helped by human resource specialists and lawyers,

receiver is individual worker, medium is writing, opportunity for feedback is questions could be asked

by letter or by requesting a meeting with direct manager or human resource manager. This would

need to be stated clearly in the letter.

Letter advantages include for legal reasons, redundancy needs to be formally stated in a letter,

whichever primary method communication is used, the wording can be made clear and easy to

understand, it is a permanent legal record of redundancy, it can be re-read and thought about carefully over a period of time before questions, questions may be individually asked and

answered.

Letter disadvantages include it may seem impersonal to employees who may resent it, especially after

long service, letter to a lot of employees may arrive through the postal system on different days, for example,

email isn't usually well received and not all employees may have email, email is sometimes not a

legally enforceable or valid means of communication, the written interchange of questions are answers

can be very long, the language used may be formal and this may make it seems even more impersonal

and uncaring, so some employees may not understand formal language.

XIII

Leadership style

Q1 Explain the types of leadership style Pierre and Oscar most closely represent.

The type of leadership style of Oscar partner who represents autocratic style at Le Menu catering business.
Autocratic leadership style features include leader takes all decisions, gives little information to staff,
supervises workers closely, only one way communication and workers only given limited information about
the business.

Oscar is a tough, direct manager, who tells workers exactly what he wants and then expects them always
to meet his high standards. If not, he is quick to let them know; he has a reputation for dismissing temporary
workers part way through an event. Oscar takes the lead during events.

Pierre is much calmer, preferring to consult with his staff.

Pierre is more involved with strategy.

Pierre works with Le Menu's chefs on the type of food to prepare for any event.

The type of leadership style of Pierre partner who represents democratic style at Le menu catering business.

Democratic leadership style features include participation encouraged, two way communication used,

which allows feedback from staff and workers given information about the business to allow full staff

involvement.

Q2 Analyze the possible reasons why Le Menu overspends on food.

The possible reasons why Le Menu overspend on food include the chefs suggest the menu who are not the ones

who control quotes or are responsible for managing the budget, if it employs one costing controller to control

every new menu quotes budget to limit it's overspend, it won't overspend on food in possible;

perhaps most of its food suppliers are expensive to provide food menu for it usually ; quotes may be done by

Oscar partner, whereas it is Pierre partner who works on the menu to do catering operation and management

job in this restaurant. If their communication is poor, the quote and menu may not match; overspends on

food will occur in accident of wrong factors from staffs and these two partners co-operation inefficiently;

quotas are for five course meals with canapes foods and drinks, this may not be fully reflected in the price

because these foods and drinks exclude the other different kind of foods purchase and so who may spend more than the quoted cost. Owing it decide to buy the other different kind of foods which have not compared

the quotes for the food suppliers before.

Q3 Discuss the advantages and disadvantaged to Le Menu of Oscar's style of leadership.

The advantages to Le Menu of Oscar's style of leadership include as below:

(a) Events are probably high pressure . In these circumstances, one person may need to take urgent decisions for

instant action, as Oscar partner manage this restaurant business by himself who don't need to discuss with

Pierre partner to spend much time to make decision to deal any matters. For example,

Oscar is a direct manager, who tells workers exactly what he wants and then expects them always

to meet his high standards in restaurant.

(b) Temporary staff (new or old staff) are not all experienced in working together and it may need a lot of

firm direction. He has a reputation for dismissing temporary workers part way through an event. Oscar takes the

lead during events. Thus, Oscar partner can help his restaurant to reduce salary to pay to the low cooking skill

of temporary chefs and low service standard of waiters etc staff when he feel their working performance can't

achieve his expectation and he shall dismiss them immediately. For long term, salary expenditure must be

reduced from his management skill.

(c) There will be no question about who is in charge or what to do. Oscar is this restaurant only manager to

let all staff to know who supervise their job and they need to listen their command how to do every job

to achieve whose expectation clearly. So, one to one communication is more easily between Oscar and

his staffs. During another partner Pierre has no authority to control and manage restaurant. Hence,

Oscar partner won't conflict with another partner Pierre often because who doesn't enquire whose opinion

how to manage restaurant staffs and operations daily.

(d) Partner Oscar can lead whose waiters service and cooker staffs to co-operate efficiently because who is a

direct manager, who tells workers exactly what he wants and then expects them always to meet his high

performance standard. Otherwise, he will dismiss them. Thus he must keep the high performance standard

of staffs to continue work in his restaurant to raise the reputation of Le Menu restaurant to every clients.

However, Oscar leadership style also has these disadvantages as below:

(a) Oscar's reputation may stop good workers wanting to work for him because who is a direct manager, who

need to tell workers exactly what he wants and then expects them always to meet his high standards. If not, he

is quick to let them know; he has a reputation for dismissing temporary workers part way through an event.

So the quality of service may fall, because who will dismiss his temporary or contract staffs easily when

he feels who are not the right staff to do the job.

(b) He may de-motivate workers, leading to lack of enthusiasm or lower productivity and the catering
    business won't be able to operate if he can't find staffs willing to work for him.

(c) Valuable ideas that come from workers may be ignored from Oscar boss. Thus, this catering restaurant will
    be difficult to develop to expand its catering service in the future.

(d) Communication channels may be blocked by unwillingness to talk to Oscar boss if his staffs are unwilling
    to reflect whose ideas to Oscar what who feel need to help when who deal these daily job to feel difficult, it will
    influence their team co-operation efficiently, e.g. if waiters or chefs teams co-operation can't be efficient,
    it will cause it's clients need to wait more time to eat and who will feel unhappy to complaint them, even
    client numbers will decrease during to this reason in the future.

XIV

Motivation

Q1 Explain what you understand by the terms:
  a. motivation
  Motivation means the intrinsic and extrinsic factors that stimulate people to take actions that lead to achieving
  a goal. Intrinsic motivation comes from satisfaction derived from working on and completing a task. Otherwise,
  extrinsic motivation comes from external rewards with working on a task, e. g. payment and other benefits.

b. responsibility
  This is the accountability for successful completion of a task /project or achievement of a goal / objective.
  It is accompanied by the authority (power) to make decisions , but either carries the bad result of things go
  wrong or carries the good result of things go right.
  Q2 Identify two factors that seem to influence job satisfaction and explain them in terms of Maslow's
  hierarchy of needs.

Maslow's Hierarchy of needs which assumes that what

motivates people is unmet needs. According to
Maslow, the needs that motivate people fall into five basic categories:
Physiological needs are the most basic need, physiological needs are the ones required for survival,
then is security needs involve keeping oneself free from harm, next is social needs are the desire for love,
friendship and companionship, esteem needs are the need for self esteem and the respect of others,
the final level is the self actualization needs(the highest level need), it describes the desire to live up to
one's full potential. People may be seeking to meet than one category of needs at a time.

These factors that seem to influence job satisfaction: For example, sense of achievement of job satisfaction
and opportunity to develop new skills are belonged to the self actualisation needs level;
recognition of work well done of job satisfaction, e.g. status, responsibility, reward is the esteem needs level;
working in teams/groups with good communication and making workers feel involved of job
satisfaction is the social needs level; contract of employment with job stability of job satisfaction is the
safety needs level; income is from employment of job satisfaction is the physical needs and esteem need
level.

Q3 Explain in terms of the features of job enrichment why it might be easier for small firms to motivate
staff than big businesses.

Job enrichment aims to use the full capabilities of workers

by giving them the opportunity to do move
challenging and fulfilling work. It may be easier for small firms to motivate because:

Job enrichment which might be easier for small firms to motivate staff than big businesses, the reasons
include wider responsibilities may be given these are fewer employees to perform tasks.

Large organizations employ many staff, it is more difficult to give them the opportunity to do move
challenging and fulfilling work for any staff motivation ; small organizations of each employee may have
to fulfil several functions, but large organizations of each employee may more difficult to have to
fulfil several functions ; small organizations of full capabilities of each employee may be more personally
and individually recognized and used to compare to large organizations of full capabilities of each employee.

Q4 Discuss the extent to which it might be possible for large firms to use Herzbeng's motivation to
improve the level of work motivation.

Herzbeng's motivations mean these are factors that results in job satisfaction. They include five match
factors as achievement, recognition for achievement, the work itself, responsibility and advancement
factors.

It might be possible for large firms to use Herzbeng's motivation to improve the level of work motivation
reasons are as employee's achievement is possible as below:

The chance of long term service is as the job uses all of the employee's capabilities fully

in large organization is more than small organization; employees' achievement may be recognised by both

financial and non financial reward from large firms whose chance is more than small firms. Because large

organization can give more chance of financial motivation may include salary or wage increases and bonuses

and chance of non financial motivation may include job enrichment and job enlargement and team working and

empowerment and interest in the work itself can be a significant motivation, e.g. large firms may offer more

scope in technical, scientific or specialist work to whose staff of chance is more than small firms.

Large organizations can have more responsibility to improve the level of work motivation. Responsibility

can be a motivator even it doesn't lead to advancement, e.g. caring, medical, pharmaceutical, law, accounting

etc professional jobs, the large organizational professional staffs need more safety and security feeling

are more than the small organizational professional staffs.

There may be more opportunity for advancement in larger firms through growth (organic or external) and

staff turnover and the fact that large firms usually have many levels of hierarchy through which on

employee can move. Thus, Herzbeng's motivation improves the level of work motivation can use in

large organizations in possible.

However, it also might not be possible for large firms to use Herzbeng's motivation to improve the level of
work motivation as below:

The reasons include that achievement may be limited within the job description, bigger firms have less
flexibility, recognition for achievement may be limited as in big firms, the recognition process may be
highly bureaucratic and slow. The work itself may be below the aptitude of the workers, e.g. graduates.

Responsibility may be limited to the job description and advancement may be slow to come and there may be
a lot of competition for higher position.

XV

organizational culture

Q1 Explain on possible reason why Sally thought it necessary to change the organizational culture of
Regal Supermarkets.

Organizational culture is the values, attitudes and beliefs of people working in an organization that control
the way they interact with one another and with external stakeholder groups.

Sally is had experience in the USA as Walmart's chief food buyer who needs to manager this UK largest
owned chain of supermarket. In fact, she can't accept this UK Regal supermarket organizational culture
so, she uses her USA organizational culture to manage this supermarket.

The possible reason why Sally thought it necessary to

change the organizational culture of

Regal Supermarkets include that she hoped Regal supermarket can become a highly competitive national

marketplace where consumers want low prices and fresh goods to attempt to make more profit, to rise

shareholder value after it is sold into a public limited company, to change it's low prices and fresh goods

image, to discourage promotion based on long service and loyalty rather than on ability and results.

Q2 Outline the type of culture that Sally seems to be introducing at Regal Supermarkets.

Autocratic leadership style features include leader takes all decisions, gives little information to staff,

supervises workers closely, only one way communication and workers only given limited information about

the business.

Sally seems to be autocratic leadership style to manage Regal Supermarkets. It includes the following feature:

Power is concentrated among a few people and decisions can be made quickly because there are few people

involved in making them because who dismisses 50% of the directors and key managers who

had been replaced and staff salary pension scheme was replaced for new recruits with flexible pay and

conditions contracts. Staff turnover increased sharply. Thus, managers are judged by result.

Sally tries to adapt the organizational culture of Regal Supermarket business to allow to be successfully

in a highly competitive national marketplace where consumers want low prices and fresh foods.

Thus, hierarchical structures are usually typical of power cultures and motivational methods are

likely to focus on financial incentives and bonuses for exceptional performance which can encourage

risky and inappropriate decision. These behaviours are an autocratic style leader personal feature.

Q3 Analyze the key steps that Sally should have taken to manage cultural change

more effectively.

Sally had experience in the USA as Walmart's chief food buyer. Currently, she

needed to manage UK Regal Supermarket which is UK one chain of supermarket

stores public limited company. Sally must need to change USA business culture to

accept UK business culture to manage this supermarket. I shall recommend that She should to take

these steps to manage cultural change if who wanted to manage this supermarket more effectively.

Before this UK supermarket organizational culture was like to a big family because Regal supermarkets

has established a culture among its staff that had contributed to its success and growth, loyalty to

family managers was very high, promotion was based on long service and loyalty, customer service

was a priority, it never intended to be the cheapest shop.

But Sally dismissed many directors and key managers, suppliers' terms were shorten, staff salary and pension scheme was replaced for new recruits with flexible pay and conditions contracts. Staffs turnover increased sharply. Sally's new organizational management changing will influence the old UK staffs can't accept happily.

Thus, the first step, I recommend Sally needed to enlarge on existing positive aspects of the supermarket business to let these old UK staffs to know why who decided to do these changing and whether what the benefits would give to these old and new staffs in the future. It aimed to make who to get confidence to work continually and who won't choose to work in another supermarkets.

The second step, Sally needed to obtain commitment of people at the top level to assist who to manage any departments in this supermarket business. Otherwise, Sally needed to replace them if they did not give full support.

The third step, Sally needed to establish new objectives and mission statement and she needed to communicate to all staffs and encouraged bottom up communication to let them to know what the future direction is and how Sally hoped her staffs needed to follow organizational policy to do daily jobs efficiently.

The fourth step, Sally needed to train old and new staffs in new methods to adapt new organizational cultural changing.

The final step, Sally needed to change staffs reward system to reward based on new value.

Q4 To what extent will the change in culture guarantee future success for this business?

Sally changes this business old culture, this supermarket will get these benefits probably as that

higher profitability makes success more likely because Sally plans try to achieve this supermarket

to be successful in a highly competitive national marketplace where consumers want low

prices and fresh goods from another new management cultural methods, emphasis on performance

is more likely to have the business running efficiently because Sally can decide to dismiss any staffs

easily if who feels their performance are not excellent , so staffs will ensure to work carefully,

decisions can be made very quickly when needed because Sally can dismiss directors and key managers

easily who are the top level staffs, so Sally don't need to discuss anyone when who plans to do any matter,

low skilled personal may benefit from autocratic management because whose each salary is also low, Sally

won't choose to dismiss them easily. Otherwise, the high skilled personal , such as managers and directors

who will be dismissed easily because whose each salary is high, so Sally dismisses them to avoid to reduce

more salary expenditure for long term benefit to supermarket.

However, sally's new organizational management culture can not ensure this supermarket will future success

and it is never guaranteed, so Sally ought to bring a USA expert into this UK supermarket who may be resented because these UK old staffs have been moved from a niche market concentrating on service and family organizational culture to adapt Sally USA organizational management culture in the future.

XVI

Organizational agreement

Q1 Explain what is meant by:

a. single union deal (or agreement)

This is an arrangement to an employer recognises only one union for purposes of collective bargaining.

Negotiations may therefore be simplified, as there won't be a diverse range of employee opinions in the negotiation.

b. collective bargaining

This is the negotiation between employee's representatives (trade unions) and employers and their representative on issues of common interest such as salary/wage payment and conditions of work. As the employees are represented as a joint force there is strengths in numbers and individual workers are less likely to be victimised for standing up for their rights.

Q2 Analyze two potential benefits to both workers and employees of a globalise union.

Swedish journalise Thomas Larsson , in his book "The Race To The Top: The real story of

Globalization (2001), stated that globalization is the process of world distance getting shorter,

things moving closer. It pertains to the increasing ease with which somebody on one side of the

world can interact, to mutual benefit, with somebody on the other side of the world.

The potential benefits to both workers and employees of a globalise union include that:

(a) A globalise union has more powerful collective bargaining power and it gives

globalization of worker rights because trade union leaders are worried by the

growth of globalisation that has weakened their power and reduce their

membership. Because employers can now easily transfer production to low cost countries, the

unions' power to bargain and negotiate higher pay deals has been much weakened.

However, a globalise trade union would be able to negotiate with multinationals on behalf of

members throughout the world and this might prevent worker exploitation in very low

wage economies.

It allows negotiation with multinationals to present transfer of production to low cost

countries and exploitation of worker and it stops companies making changes to pay/

rights in one country without consulting workers in other countries.

Thus a globalise union can threaten to global companies (employers) to treat to pay
the unreasonable salaries/wages to whose staffs and workers unfairly.

(b) A globalise trade union challenges the global forces of capital to raise more job opportunities
to different countries workers and employees to get jobs to do more easily because a globalise
trade union encourage any local companies to expand to overseas to do multinational businesses.
Thus, one country workers and employees can have more job opportunities to move to another
country to work if the local company expanded to overseas to do multinational company business
and globalise trade union is the middleman role to solve conflicts between any multinational employers and
employees and workers when the employees and workers need it to help any time.

Reference
Thomas Larsson, The Race to the Top: The real story of globalization(US: Cato Institute,
2001), p.9

Q3 To what extent would any one multinational company be likely to be affected by the
development of one large global trade union?
The reasons would be significant for any one multinational company be likely to be affected by the

development of one large global trade union include that :

(a) One large global trade union could standardise of payment and work conditions, it could lead any one

multinational company to pay higher costs and less competitiveness, therefore a multinational company could

not take so much competitive advantage of cheap labour, which could seriously affect profit.

Any one multinational company could not pay the most minimum labour salaries/wages to its employees in any

countries easily, if one large global trade union developed to standardise of payment and work conditions

to protect any countries employees to have the reasonable salaries/wages standard level and improved safe

work environment in factories or offices or shops or warehouses working locations etc.

In consequence, any one multinational company would spend more expenditure to labour salaries/wages and

any one multinational company also needed to rise expenditure to improve whose working environment to

be safety to every employee. Thus, any one multinational company's profit would be reduced largely.

(b) Negotiations may take longer and include a lot more international involvement between any one

multinational company and it's employees and workers.

(c) Every country's any one multinational company 's employer and employees issues could also

change into a worldwide problem more easily.

(d) One set of negotiations may be a lot simpler than different negotiations in lots of different

countries from a globalise trade union.

(e) Any one multinational company acquisition or merger would mean a constant stream of change,

which could complicate the whole process and interfere with external growth.

(f) Different local costs of living may be very difficult to take into account for any one multinational

company.

(g) A globalise trade union reduces the power of a multinational company over its workforce.

The reasons would also be little or no effect on any one multinational company be likely to be affected by the

development of one large global trade union include that :

(a) In practical terms, different local laws and living costs may take the process very difficult to put into

effect to any one multinational company because different local law and living costs are external factor

to influence to any one multinational company indirectly.

(b) In a recession unions may be happy to have jobs for their workers, so may not take advantage of

global negotiating power to any one multinational company directly.

(c) Job losses in one country could lead another new job to another country when any one multinational company does local and overseas business both.

In conclusion, I believe that it is significant for any one multinational company be likely to be affected by the
development of one large global trade union. The reason is that multinational firms exist because certain
economic conditions make in possible for any one multinational company to profitability undertake production
of a product or service in a foreign location. Production of a product or service in foreign market is desirable in
the presence of protectionist barriers, high transportation costs, unfavourable currency exchange
rate shifts or requirement for local adoption to local demand that make exporting from the
home country unfeasible or unprofitable.

XVII

crisis management

Q1 Define the following terms:

a. Crisis management

A crises goes beyond the normal and causes instability or imposes a change in an organization and it can

threaten its future. The impacts of a crisis are therefore experienced across an organization and the

response requires strategic lead in order to (attempt to) manage and control or direction of events.

Thus, a crisis is a form of sudden impact which happens with little or no warning to any organizations.

The origins of a crisis can either be external , where the organization is seen as a victim of an event

beyond its control (e.g. natural disasters) or internal , where a crisis occurs due to accidents in the

workplace (e.g. technical errors) or due to systemic, preventable errors (e.g. human breakdown

accidents, organizational misleads causing injury, or the occurrence of a situation that is outside the current capacity and experience of the management team, as a result of , for

example, key personnel not being available at a particular point in time).

Crisis management is a term often used to describe the way in which cay organization can handle a crisis.

It is planning relates to get the best position to react to and recover from an emergency, incident reacts

properly and orderly to an incident as it occurs.

Thus, organizations need good crisis management plan to reduce much losses when any crisis occurs.

b. contingency plan

A plan is used by an organization or business unit to respond to a specific systems failure or disruption

of operations.

An organization concentrate on using contingency plan to minimize loss and ensure continuity of the

critical business functions of it in the event of disaster.

It is process of developing advance arrangement and procedures that enable an organization to respond

to an event that could occur by chance or unforeseen circumstances.

Q2 Outline the key steps BP would have gone through to produce a contingency plan

for a crisis such as the Deepwater Horizon.

The British petroleum (BP) company Gulf of Mexico disaster occurred on 20 April , 2010 year, the Deepwater

Horizon drilling rig exploded , killing 11 workers and causing an oil spill that soon became the worst environmental disaster. If it had produced a contingency plan for any crisis, I believe that the Deepwater Horizon disaster would not happen easily.

I shall recommend these key steps for it to produce a contingency plan to reduce any business and life loss from any crisis occurrence in the future as below:

The first step, BP company needs to have strong safety culture. It is the set of values held by employees and it's policies that lead employees to prioritize health, safety and the working environment. Many policies and procedures can affect a Deepwater drilling firm's safety culture and thereby affect employees' actions that could cause a spill. Hence, the top level staffs of chief executive officer and managers to the low level staffs of drilling petrol workers can learn BP safety culture how to work in their working environment safely.

BP can produce a risk analysis to measure all workers whose work environment whether is safe or dangerous in order to permit where their working environment is safe for them to work.

The second step, it needs to produce a crisis communication, it means there are lessons to be learned to all employees about not only what could have been done to prevent the spill of drilling rig accident occurrence, but about how to combat an environment crisis on the public relations. For example, a crisis response strategy is needed to implemented by the BP on Twitter internet media. It aims to achieve effective in using social media to control the public relations. Crisis that resulted from the explosion and oil spill, people will respond and react on social media outlets. Hence, social media is as a platform to express opinion and attitude in the BP oil spill

response and BP can collect more useful crisis handling methods to reduce the disaster of accidents occur again.

The final step, BP needs to provide training to workers to rise their skills to use different equipments and using

a compensation structure that encourage individuals to make decisions that increase safety. Upper management

ought need to implement internal policies that affect safety culture and makes decisions and lower level

managers and other employees respond to incentives created by upper management create a link between safe

culture and safe outcomes.

Q3 Analyze the reasons why the BP share price fell by 50 % following the Deepwater Horizon crisis.

After the Deepwater Horizon, explosion disaster occurred on April , 2010 year. It had caused the bad news to

BP. The bad news included that BP announced to compensate $20 billion amount to victims of the oil spill and

it would not pay every shareholder dividend in 2010 year. Hence, investors would feel it had finance difficult

and shareholders felt BP would have loss because who could not receive dividend in 2010 year. It caused

it's future shareholders lose confidence to invest to buy its shares, even it's old shareholders would sell their

shares immediately. When it's share numbers were decreasing, it would also reduce it's share price fall by 50% seriously.

Q4 Discuss the likely benefits and limitations of BP's contingency planning when preparing for any future disasters like Deepwater Horizon.

The benefits and limitations of BP's contingency planning when prepare for future disaster as below:

The likely benefits of BP's contingency planning can include that:

(a) It will reduce the chance of drilling ring exploding occurrence again.

(b) It will rise the confidence to it's new and old shareholders to continue to invest to it's oil productive

business for long term.

(c) It's employees will have confidence to work in its drilling oil rig working environment when who

feel their working environment is more safe to work. Otherwise, if it's employees felt who were unsafe

to work in its work environment who would leave BP easily , specially, BP's experienced skilful workers

would leave BP and found another new employer.

(e) It will build loyalty to public because corporate social responsibility is becoming of great importance and

consumers consider more than just its petrol products quality and price when making a purchase.

(f) Understanding exacting how the oil spill was caused and the extent of the damages that resulted, including

damages to the natural environment, economy and citizens' health and well being provided evidence as to

why people were to dismay by the spill and processing the knowledge that it would have been prevented

with some basic safety precaution.

Hence, if it produced a contingency plan, it could give public to have confidence to continue to buy its shares to

invest to help it to do business in the future.

However, BP would likely encounter these limitations to implement it's contingency planning as below:

(a) The failure of the America government to assign and in some cases to permit resources to assist

with the containment of the oil spill. Although, it can get these benefits from the contingency planning,

but it still lacks enough funds to repurchase any advanced and safe oil spill productive equipments.

(b) It needs to spend much time and expenditure to provide training to help it's old and new skilful

workers to learn how to control oil spilling equipments easily to reduce human error and

equipments failure in the short time.

(c) The disaster crisis would have been avoided if proper safe precautions were taken.

For example, reducing drilling Deepwater Horizon to be evacuated overnight to cause

fire occurrence chance to the incident. In fact, BP lacked enough skilful workers and

equipments, so it's workers need to work overnight to cause fire.

In conclusion, BP's contingency planning will likely to get these benefits, but it needs to

have more fund to repurchase many advanced oil spilling equipments and paid more

expenditure to provide training to raise it's skilful workers knowledge to control these

new equipments if it wanted to get the benefits from contingency planning in fact.

XVIII

Company define

Q1 Define the terms:

a. Public limited company

A public limited company needs to issue shares from public shares exchange market to carry on selling shares

to public to get share capital to shareholders.

Liability (loans) of a public limited company is limited and directors and shareholders are separate legal

personal liable to company's loans. It means a company is a legal person which can be sued to pay any

compensation to shareholders or lenders, e.g. bank or trade suppliers or creditors for any losses or loans.

b. Share price

Every public limited company can control and decide share price by itself when it issues it's shares to

shares exchange market to sell to public to become it's shareholders.

Share price can be changed (fluctuated) to be rose or fallen down. For example: when the public limited company can earn profit, it is possible that it's share price will be influenced to rise.

Otherwise, when it had loss, it is possible that it's share price will be influence to be fall down

in the shares exchange market.

Q2 Outline two possible sources of long term finance available to Easy Jet.

I shall recommend why bank loan or mortgage and issuing shares are the best source of long term finance to it.

Easy Jet is Europe's second largest low fare airline, it is privately owned by Mr Haji Ioannon owner and

chief executive, who and brother and sister owned 75% shares to control company operation.

Easy Jet's decision to buy new aircrafts (fixed assets) to addition of new Boeing 737-700s airlines 32 numbers

and opening new routes can be seen as an attempt to protect and build on their current position.

Banks were going particularly interested in the company to lend loans to increase its capital. Bank would have

confidence to lend to it to invest because Easy Jet can have enough cash to prepare to buy 32 aircraft numbers

and it was a private own limited company, the owner has 75% share ownership. So, bank would believe

Mr Haji Ioannon was the major shareholder who had enough capital to operate airline business and who had

ability to pay bank loans after bank lent loan to him and Easy Jet could had earned profit and it's share price

had raised. Thus, it had more possible that banks would be willing to lend large amount of long term

finance to him.

The another long term finance source is to issue new shares to public to increase capital. Easy Jet share price
had raised 10% per share. It issued $63 million shares, it has raised to $195 million capital and it's market
valued has reached to $328 million. It would make public have confidence to buy its shares to invest to its
business for long term. Hence, it is right time, it ought choose to issue much shares to increase shareholder
numbers to help it to raise long term finance.

Q3 Explain why an expansion in Easy jet's passenger numbers has increased the need for short and long
term finance.

I shall indicate the reasons why Easy Jet airline expands to increase passengers which needs long and short term
finance.

The short term finances include bank overdraft, short term bank loan and creditors etc finance source.

It needs short term finances to help it to pay new employees, new office rent, electricity, maintenance etc new
office general expenditure. During it expands to Europe overseas airline markets, it needs to open new office
in Europe different countries. So, it needs to pay more expenditure to Europe different countries. Even,
it needs to increase expenditure to spend television, radio and internet advertisement to promote it's airline
business to let Europe different countries passengers to know the benefits who can give if who choose to
book Easy Jet airline to fly. Hence, an expansion to Europe routes to increase passenger numbers, Easy Jet
airline needs to increase the short term finance to pay this Europe different countries new office expenditure.

The long term finances include long term bank loan or

mortgage, even issuing debentured or shares to public to
buy in share exchange market. The reason is that Easy
Jet airline's strategy is largely expanding upon existing
capacities in operating a low cost airline. Expanding to
pay the fleet of aircraft numbers potentially offers cost
efficiency advantages in terms of economies of scale and
scope across s bigger number of routes. Standardising
on new Boeing 737-300s and 737-700s aircrafts (fixed
assets) should also help to minimise operational costs as
well as the purchase economies from the deal discount.

However, Easy Jet's decision to buy new aircrafts (fixed
assets) to addition of 32 numbers of new Boeing
737-700s aircrafts, it must need to spend much
expenditure to buy these aircrafts to help it to carry many
passengers to Europe different countries' new routes
and opening new routes can be seen as an attempt position.

Thus, it must need to lend long term finance to pay
aircraft suppliers to buy these aircrafts if it wanted to
expand to Europe overseas airline markets to increase
passenger numbers successfully.

Q4 Evaluate the view that Easy jet's decision to raise long
term finance by selling shares is preferable
to raising it through borrowing.

Although Easy Jet airline have many choices to get long
term finance. For example: long term bank loan or
mortgage or debenture, trade creditors etc. However,
issuing shares to get finance choice is preferable than
other choices. I shall indicate the reasons as below:

(a) In fact, selling shares can give these benefits to Easy Jet
airline. Firstly, it doesn't need to pay bank loan and
interest to the banks every year if it doesn't choose to
borrow long term loan from banks.

Supposed it issued a lot of numbers of new share to the London share exchange market and there are many

buyers plan to choose to buy it's shares. After they buy Easy Jet shares, if its shareholders have confidence that

it would continue to gain profit and its share price would rise and it would increase dividend, who won't willing

to sell their shares easily and would keep shares for long term investment. Hence, Easy Jet airline must have

afford capital to buy any new aircrafts(fixed assets) or paying advertisement and new office rent etc

expenditure to expand to Europe overseas airline markets.

(b) If Easy Jet airline chose to issue shares to raise long term finance. I believe that it could possible to sell

many shares to increase much cash capital in the short term.

The reason is that the background of Easy Jet airline was a famous private owned British discount airfare

limited company, was established in 1995 year by Stelios Haji Ioannon owner and whose brother and

sister (directors) owned 75% shares to their company. Thus they were major this company major shareholders

to own this company capital to invest to Easy Jet airline. Moreover, it's share price had raised 10% per share

and issued $63 million shares, it had raised to $195 million capital. It's market valued has reached to

$328 million. It implied that the shareholders were increasing every year and there were many investors had

interest to buy its shares in the future.

It provided scheduled passenger airline services and started operations with two leased Boeing 737-200 aircrafts. Initially operating for London to Glasgow UK routes. In the subsequent year, it expanded to

Aberdeen and another rotes in UK (Datamonitor, 2012, p.6).

In the early 2000 year, it became listed on the London stock exchange and further expanded its route network

across Europe. It set up multiple bases of airport in countries, such as Germany, France, Spain and Italy

effectively to presence in Europe. Moreover, airbus became Easy Jet's preferred aircraft suppliers and long

term purchase orders were placed (Datamonitor, 2012, p.6).

Easy jet airline aimed to become Europe's leading short haul airline by making air travel simple and affordable

and it solely utilized airbus aircraft to fly its routes, giving it flexibility to change capacity amounts and to

capitalize on appearing opportunities. It had driven increased revenue through its internet, television and

mobile marketing to enter European airline market (Easy Jet plc, 2012, p.14).

In conclusion, owing to Easy Jet airline past business performance was very good, so it could earn profit

seriously. It would case future investors have more confidence to buy its shares to help it to expand to

Europe airline markets for long term. Thus, I agree that Easy Jet airline ought choose to issue shares to sell to

raise long term finance is preferable to raising finance from borrowing loan from banks.

Reference

Datamonitor (2012, Feb.9). Easy Jet plc: Company profile. Retrieved from http://www.datamonitor.com/

Easy Jet Plc (2012).Annual report. Retrieved from http://2012annualreport.easyjet.com/downloads/PDFS/ Full-annual_Report_2012.pdf

XIX

Finance define

Q1 Define the following terms:

a. residual value

Residual value means the estimate sale or scrape value of a fixed asset at the end of its useful lifespan after the

companies' the fixed asset which is estimated accumulation depreciation period to the end of useful period.

Either if the asset's sale value is more than the scrap value, it will show the gain of the asset sold to the profit

and loss account or if the asset's sale value is less than the scrape value, it will show the loss of the asset sold

to the profit and loss account in the company's financial report.

b. expected life expectancy

Expected life expectancy means the length of time that a fixed asset will probably be useful and productive

to a business before it is sold as scrape or replaced. Thus, the asset will be depreciated to estimate it's period

that which can be used and produced to a business.

Q2 Explain how Asia Print might have forecast future annual sales.

The Asia print plc is a large printing firm offering a range of service to industry, such as printed catalogues,

leaflets and brochures to business clients. It operates in a vary competitive printing market, it is easy for

new firms to join using the latest computer software page making packages.

It can use sales trend analysis method to forecast future annual sales to measure its competitive ability in this

printing service market.

Firstly, by taking prior year sales performance offering a range of service to industry, such as printed

catalogues, leaflets and brochures to business clients all one year printing service income. Then adjusting

it's prior year printing service income for future economic and/or industry forecasts together with expected

changes in fashion or demand, even it is possible needs to research or gather it's competitors' offering printing

service market data.

Finally, it needs to move averages trend analysis to take account of seasonal variations to forecast future annual

offering printing service income. For example, if it's country economy would be predicted better next year, it

implied there would have more different industries, the businessmen would need to find people to help them to

print catalogues, brochures and office documents etc service due to their businesses are more and they have no

more time to do printing job, who need to find people to help them to print a lot of documents.

Thus, it needs to search next year competitors' offering printing service market data and predicating

it's businessmen client numbers based on current year printing service income to forecast future printing
service income per year.

Q3 Calculate for each project:
a. the payback period
Given data Project Y Project Z

Purchase (P) price in printing machine $20 million $12 million
Life expectancy in years (Y) 5 4
Sales forecast units (U) 8 million units 6 million units
sale (S) price per item $1.25 $1.25
Variable (V) cost per unit $0.5 $0.5
Annual (a) operating cost in $1 million $0.5 million
Cash flow forecasts for project Y printing machine
Calculation per year net cash flow amount: u (s less v)
less (a) = $(8 million x 0.75) less $1 million
=$5 million
Year Cash flow Cumulative cash flow
0 -$(20) million -$(20) million
1 $5 million -$(15) million
2 $5 million -$(10) million
3 $5 million -$(5) million
4 $5 million 0 = payback period
Total net cash flow $5 million $5 million
Thus, payback period is 4 year for project Y.

Cash flow forecasts for project Z printing machine
Calculation per year net cash flow amount: u (s less v)
less (a) = $(6 million x 0.75) less $0.5 million
=$4 million
Year Cash flow Cumulative cash flow

0 -$(12) million -$(12) million
1 $4 million -$(8) million
2 $4 million -$(4) million
3 $4 million 0=pay back period
4 $4 million $4 million
Total net cash flow $4 million $4 million
Thus, payback period is 3 year for project Z.

b. the average annual rate of return (ARR)
ARR project Y = (Total net cash flow add residual value) / number of years
=($5 million + $1 million) / 5
=$1.2 million per annum
ARR project Z = (Total net cash flow add residual value) / number of years
=($4 million + $0.5 million)/4
=$1.125 million per annum

Q4 On the basis of your results and any other relevant factors, discuss which project Asia
Print should choose.
Basis of my results and any other relevant factors, I shall recommend which project Asia Print Plc should
choose project Y.
I shall use comparison of these factors to decide why Asia Print Plc to choose project Y is better than project Z
to gain more benefits.
Financial factors project Y project Z Comment Which project
is better?
Total cash flow $ 5 million $ 4 million Bigger cash flow is better Y

Project length 5 years 4 years Shorter means less risk of Z
unknown changes in the
market
Payback period 4 years 3 years Shorter payback is less risky Z

ARR $2.2 million $1.6 million Higher ARR is preferable Y
Non financial factors
(quality factors)
Machine Considerable Considerable Both equal disruption Y/Z
disruption to disruption to
change change
new, not prove proven reliability is important Z
reliability reliability
features highly automated, semi-
fast change over, automated Automated means Y/Z
full colour, direct more than go wrong
internet to customers but quality may be better

none noisy: complaints are not good Y
residents may
complain
staff two staffs would existing staff training is expensive, Z
need selection and can operate staff may leave when who is
training trained to work in project Z
six staffs three staffs redundancies are caused Z
are redundancies and are and unions are
union worried redundancies problematic
about job cuts

In conclusion, there are factors for and against both project Y and project Z to choose which is either more

benefits. However, project Z has the slight advantages on the number of factors, it has in its favour, but

these factors are not weighted. it does after all, represent lower technology which may not be as competitive

in the future.

However, because project Y printing machine is highly automated, fast change over, full colour, direct

internet to customers, but project Z printing machine is semi-automated and it can produce noisy it

is printing, it will cause residents complain when it helps clients to print their brochures or documents in

its office, so the calm environment will be produced noise to influence residents' living close to its office.

Even, project Z's payback period and project length is shortened than project Y, it is not the major benefits

to Asia print Plc for the long term. Thus, project Y can give more benefits to Asia Print Plc possibly.

XX

Loan finance

Q1 Define the following terms:

a. loan finance

Loan finance can comprise either short term (under one year) or long term (over one year) borrowing. It can

be sourced from banks, other businesses e.g. finance companies or business investors who give finance to lend

loan to company to do its business. Loan finance may be secured or unsecured. Secured loan means that the

lender would be largely entitled to take and sell the secured assets if lender needed a payment of loan interests

or capital repayment, but the loan borrower (loan company can't pay to the lender).

b. liquidity

Liquidity means the ability of a firm to pay its short term debts. It is analyzed by examining working capital

(current assets less current liabilities) and the current ratio (current assets/ current liabilities). If working

capital is positive and the current ratio is much than 1, than the business is said to be liquid because it can pay all its short term liabilities by liquidating its short term assets. In reality, liquidation of assets may not achieve

full book price and so estimates of liquidity are approximate.

Q2 explain why material costs have been forecast to be 50% of sales.

I shall give reasons to indicate why coffee call plc 's material costs have been forecast to be 50% of sales.

In fact, there is no direct evidence to indicate how of 50% was arrived at.

However, my first supporting reason supposes many coffee retail businesses may make a 100% mark up on the

cost of materials. This means that the cost of coffee materials would be doubled in order to arrive at the selling

price of the coffee products. If coffee sales have been estimated for the purpose of the cash flow statement, it

would therefore be necessary to halve the coffee sales price in order to arrive at the cost of materials. The

calculation is this done in reverse.

However, forecasting coffee call plc coffee material costs 50% of sales can reduce the risk of loss if its sales

price could not reach to its predicted sale price level to achieve its coffee sale numbers.

Another reason is because coffee material costs can fluctuate to go up price. If next year, coffee material

supplying numbers reduce suddenly, the coffee material suppliers will raise their coffee material price,

if coffee call plc doesn't increase its coffee sales price because it feels client numbers will influence to

be decreased if it increase coffee sale prices next year. Thus, it will cause to earn less profit or loss possibly

and coffee material costs have been forecast to be 50% of sale is more prudence method to avoid loss occurrence for the further six months.

Q3 draw up a cash flow forecast for coffee call for the first six months of the year.

Coffee call plc

Cash flow forecast for the first six months of the year

Inflows Jan. Feb. March April May June

$000 $000 $000 $000 $000 $000

sales 20 20 20 40 40 40

loans / 20 / / / /

total in (a) 20 40 20 40 40 40

less outflows

coffee material (10) (10) (10) (20) (20) (20)

electricity/gas / (20) / / / /

wages (2) (2) (2) (3) (3) (3)

Erin & Carl / / (20) / / /

drawings

marketing (0.5) (0.5) (0.5) (0.5) (0.5) (0.5)

refit cost -

fixed asset

of furniture installation (20)

total out (b) (12.50) (32.50) (32.50) (23.50) (23.50) (23.50)

net cash flow

(a-b)

7.5 7.5 (12.50) 16.50 16.50 16.50

opening balance 7 14.50 22.00 9.50 26.00 42.50

closing balance 14.50 22.00 9.50 26.00 42.50 59.00

Q4 discuss the advantages and disadvantages of coffee call using the venture capitalist as

a source of finance

I shall indicate the advantages and disadvantages of coffee call plc coffee sale business using the venture capitalist as a source of finance.

Venture capitalist means a company that offers money to new companies or for high risk expansion in return

for a percentage share ownership.

The advantages of using the venture capitalist as source of finance as:

(a) Coffee call plc can get extra advice and experience of venture capitalist could be useful. Thus, venture

capitalist needs to provide consultant service to help it how to deal any problems when it encounters to open

this new coffee sale business in the beginning. For example: Giving suggestions to it how to promote its

different types of coffee to let clients to know in the coffee sale market, hoe to set coffee sale price to make

clients to feel reasonable and what coffee productive equipments and coffee materials of it needs to buy.

(b) The loan amount $20,000 is a sizeable sum which is only really needed for March and April and so it

could offer the possibility of further future expansion.

In fact, its cash flow forecast indicated that it has positive net cash flow amount in Jan. and Feb. two months.

Thus, it didn't borrow loans before March because it forecasted to buy coffee material amounts are double from

April to June months of this year.

(c) Share capital needs not be repaid, venture capitalist can wait it to pay share capital when it can attempt to

earn profit as well as share capital is paid for in dividends, which can be optional in other expenses make them

difficult to pay. Hence, coffee call plc can borrow venture capitalist finds to increase share capital and it can use

these cash to prepare to pay any forecast expenditures and it doesn't need to owe further future suppliers' expenditures from Jan. to June months of this year and it's this six months won't show trade creditor amounts

in balance sheet liabilities of this year six months to let the public who have more confidence to buy it's shares

in this year six months possibly.

(d) Leverage would be lower, it is less possibility of future bank finance for other projects from Jan. to June

months of this year. Thus, long term or short term bank loans amount won't be shown in this six months balance

sheet, it increase that shareholders have more confidence to buy this business shares.

(e) Cash flow forecasts are rarely certain. The extra cash could be useful if reality does not live up to

expectations. Thus venture capital loan can increase its net cash available to be prepared to pay these six

months' business expenditure certainly.

(f) Venture capitalist can be its temporary shareholders, even long term shareholders if there are not

many shareholders have confidence to buy its shares to invest to it's coffee sale business in the beginning.

It implies that venture capitalist can help it to let many shareholders have confidence to invest its business

from further Jan. to June months period. Thus, it has possible to increase many shareholder numbers in

this six months period.

However, if also has disadvantages to choose to use the venture capitalist to as a source of finance.

(a) Eric and Carl two partners borrow $20,000 amount of loans from venture capitalist in Feb. who

would be giving away 20% of the ownership when who only really need the cash if only needed for two months period. This seems a heavy price to pay to use this two months expenditure wrongly.

(b) If Eric and Carl partners simply delayed taking their own drawings for two months who would

not need to give up 20% shares of their business. Thus who borrow this venture capitalist loan ,who were

encouraged to drawing their business cash for private use within further six months.

(c) Dividends are paid after profit tax, whereas loan interest is paid before profit tax. Thus, this

venture capitalist loan increases their coffee sale business loan interest expenditure when it will start

only two months period to do this business. It is too short time to lend this loan.

(d) ROCE will be lower because the loan is started early.

In conclusion, although who chooses venture capitalist to get share capital loan to support to pay it's business

expenditure next six months, but it also has these disadvantages. However, venture capitalist can give any

useful suggestion to help it how to set up this new coffee sale business in the beginning. Thus, I feel it

is more value to compare to choose to borrow loan from bank.

XXI

Budget

Q1 Define the following terms:

a. budgeted figures

Budgeted figures are set for both sale revenues and costs and if is used to each cost and profit centre for the

forecast, it is planned that organization aim to fulfil.

Budgets include sale budgets, capital expenditure budget, labour cost budgets, material cost budgets etc. It is

not a forecast because a forecast is a prediction of what could in the future.

In conclusion, financial planning process is known as budgeting. It gives organizational real direction and

purpose and against which actual performance can be compared.

b. variances

Variance analysis is the process of investigating any difference between budget figures and actual figured. It

will get results either adverse variance, it exists when the difference between the budgeted and actual figure leads to a lower than expected profit or favourable variance, it exists when the difference between the budgeted

and actual figure leads to a higher then expected profit.

Q2 explain how a manufacturing business sets budgets for sales and costs.

Ths Oasia cookers ltd is a gas and electric ovens productive products company. It is as a manufacturing

business will sets budgets for sales and costs steps as below:

The first stage, manufacturing organization will set objectives are for the next years and these objectives based

on previous performance. For example, what happened last year forecast will influence how to set future

objectives.

The second stage, setting next year sale budget which will be based on research and past sale data.

The key or limiting factors can also influence manufacturing business sale growth budget next year.

For example, if manufacturing business current year sale budget proves to be inaccurate and setting a level that

proves to be too high, then cash, production, labour cost budgets will become inaccurate too.

Thus, the sale budget is prepared after discussion with sale managers in all branches and divisions of the

manufacturing business.

Stage third, subsidiary budgets are prepared which will base on the plans budget, administration budget,

labour cost budget, material cost budget and manufacturing distribution budget.

The budget holders, e.g. cost and profit centre managers should be involved in this process if aim of delegated

responsibility for budgets is to be achieved.

Stage fourth, a budgeting committee with ensure all sale and cost budgets don't conflict with each other and that

the spending level planned doesn't exceed the resources of manufacturing business.

Stage fifth, a master budget contains the main details of all other budgets and concludes with a budget profit

or loss to profit and loss account and balance sheet.

The final stage, the master budget is then presented to the board of directors for approval. Once, approved the

sale and cost budgets will become the basic of the operational plans of each department and cost centre.

Thus manufacturing business is sale budget must budget exactly because it will influence any cost budgets.

Q3 Complete the table by calculating the variances, indicating whether they are adverse

or favourable.

Oasis cookers Ltd

Budget figures Actual figures Variance

$'000 $'000 $'000

adverse/favourable

sales revenue 165 150 adverse-(15)

cost of material 80 70 favourable 10

labour cost 22 23 adverse -(1)

gross profit 63 57 adverse-(6)

overhead 40 43 adverse-(3)

net profit 23 14 adverse-(9)

It indicates that Oasis cookers Ltd has only cost of material has favourable variance, all sales revenue, labour

cost, gross profit, overhead and net profit have adverse favourable variances. Thus, implies it's actual

performance is worse to compare actual performance variances. It needs to find factors why it causes these adverse variances this year.

Q4 Using the variance results, comment on the performance of Oasis Cookers during the year.

I shall follow variance results to give these comment on the performance of Oasis cookers ltd during the year.

It's gross profit is adverse variance. The reasons are become labour costs (wages) rise. Although material costs

fall down but it's sale revenue is adverse variance, e.g. the client numbers decrease.

However it wants to increase gross profit, I suggest it needs to reduce sales price or/and reduce worker numbers

or reduce worker wages. Any way, it's net profit is adverse variance because overhead costs are adverse

variance. I suggest it needs to control electricity and water and general office etc expenditure to reduce their

overhead its budget.

In conclusion, my suggestions are not sure to help it to raise gross and net profits. However, if it does not

attempt to find the factors to cause its overspending, it is difficult to increase profit in the short term.

Q5 Evaluate the usefulness of budget to a business such as Oasis Cookers.

The sales and costs control budgets will be useful to this Oasis cookers Ltd manufacturing business. The

reasons are national economy is experiencing a downturn with no economic growth and government

forced to increase interest rate to control cost push inflation and caused an appreciation of currency

exchange rate. It caused that foreign even imports are falling in price. These external factors can influence

Oasis cookers ltd to make gas and electric oven numbers to sell to retailers because retailers need to reduce its oven products to export to overseas to sell, so retailers profit are also influenced to be decreased.

It's situation is such as Ford Motor. Ford Motor's car sale numbers are decreasing, it owns 2000 cost centres in

UK operations. If it had no any sale cost budget every year, it is more difficult to know the reasons why its

profit is increasing.

Thus, the sale and cost budgets can give Oasia cookers Ltd these advantages:

These budgets process can help it to set sale objectives to each overseas market to sell its gas and electric oven

products, so its product manufacturing and sale numbers are based on forecasted total budget numbers for

every overseas sale markets. It can inform to its retailers ought sell how many gas and electric oven products to

every countries every month. It will increase confidence to retailers to help it to sell its products.

Thus, it can follow the oven products actual and budget sale revenue to estimate how many ovens ought to sell

to different countries to set the best profit possibly.

Another way it's overhead actual figure is more than budgeted figure. It implied that it has overspending any

overhead expenditure. Then, it can investigate whether which kind of overhead costs actual figures are exceed

to budgeted figure and it can plan how to reduce the overspending of these kind of overhead cost as well as it's

labour costs actual figures are more than budgeted figures. It also implies that it ought to reduce some worker

numbers or reduce that wages.

In conclusion, this sale and cost budget variances analysis can help Oasis cookers Ltd to investigate whether

what the factors cause its gross and net profits are falling down from these adverse variance items figures in this budget variance analysis report.

XXII

Business cooperation advantage

Q1 List two advantages that the large supermarket chains will have over Carlo's shop.

Although, Carols Chaves is a sale trader small specialist food shop, who owns personal unique service to offer

to whose clients and his food is high quality advantages to attract whose clients to choose to buy its specialist

foods. However, large supermarket chains shall have these advantages to compete with Carlos Chaves's food

shop in this food sale market. Large supermarket chains are sun by national or multi-national retail chains.

They carry wide range of competitively price's own brand as well as branded foods. They were then also to

pass on the discount to their customers. For example, bulk transportation of foods are the most economical way of moving items from overseas import. Thus, they can sell cheap fruits to their clients in supermarkets.

Supermarkets have to work with suppliers who are local. The need to supply good quality products at low

prices means that they can't do business with farmers who don't produce good quality products in large

quantities. Thus if customers want to buy cooking foods or farming foods, supermarkets can use their

power to make sure that animal farmed for their foods have good, healthy and lives, such as organic and

farm fresh food lines. Supermarkets can bring huge benefits to local communities. Their restaurant areas

prove good meeting places for shoppers and their large car parks make shopping easier and more convenient.

Typically, supermarkets provide local sports centres, parks, play areas and better roads.

Q2 a. Prepare a trading and profit and loss account for the year ending 31 Dec. 2010.

Show all workings.

Carlo Chaves sole trader

Trading and profit & loss account for the

year ended 31 Dec. 2010 year.

$

Food sale revenues $80,000 x 12 months 960,000

less cost of foods sold $80,000 x 12 months x 75% (720,000)

Gross profit 240,000

less indirect cost $20,000 x 12 months (240,000)

0

less Depreciation of new van (fixed asset) working (i) (8,000)

Net loss - (8,000)

working (i) (New Van cost \$40,000 less sale value \$8,000) / 4 years

b. Cal. the annual dep. expense of the van.
(New Van cost \$40,000 less sale value \$8,000) / 4 years
= \$8,000

c. Discuss the usefulness of Carlos's profit and loss account to
different stakeholders.

The profit and loss account of Carlos Chave's specialist food sale business can gives these usefulness to his
different stakeholders.

Accounts are financial record of business transactions, which are needed to provide essential information to
groups both with and outside the organizations.

As this specialist food sale business financial report can help Carlos Chave (inside stakeholder, business
owner) to measure performance to compare against targets, previous time periods and competitors
(supermarkets) and it can help him to take decisions, such as opening new food shop branched or closing
Carlos's specialist food sale shop whether Carlos needs to employ staffs to help him or not. Hence, this
food sale business financial report can help Carlos to decide if it is profitable, whether it was likely to expand or
if it is making losses, whether he could lead to close this food sale business.

Carlos's financial report can also give these data to external stakeholders as below:
(a) Banks can decide whether to lend money, asses whether to allow an increase in overdraft facilities to

Carlos's food sale business.

(b) Creditors can assess whether it is secure and liquid enough to pay its debts, whether it is secure to assure of

future suppliers of foods who are purchasing.

(c) Government can calculate how much tax it is due to determine whether it is likely to expand to create more

jobs or whether it is in danger of closing down and creating economic problems and confirm it's financial report

is produced within the terms of accounting regulations legally.

In conclusion, Carlos's food sale business financial report can imply how it's food reputation (Goodwill or

business name) to it's clients' feeling and confidence in the long term. If it is a scare food that risk consumers'

health, it's business reputation can disappear very rapidly. In fact, it shows net loss of $8,000. so it implies

it's business performance is not good due to its bad reputation to clients.

XXIII

Asset define

Q1 Define the following terms:

a. current assets

Current assets mean the company owns cash on hand or in bank, closing stocks, debtors, prepaid expenses,

accrued income etc items. These current assets are owned available less than one year to show in company's

balance sheet commonly.

b. capital employed

Capital employed includes either the sole trader or partners putting cash capital, himself/herself

individual equity or partners' equity add the long term liabilities total amount.

Corporation(public or private limited company) issues shares to shareholders to buy in stock exchange market,

so corporation share capital is from the shareholders who buy its shares to get cash finance source

(shareholders equity) and add the long term liabilities total amount.

Capital employed can also calculate from fixed assets add current assets less current liabilities total amount.

Q2 Explain one ratio you would use to measure Karachi's liquidity

Karachi paper product plc is a paper sale business. I shall use liquidity ratio to measure whether it has

ability to liquidity or not.

Liquidity means it assesses the ability of the firm to pay short term debts, it relates to working capital.

If there is too little working capital, then business could become illiquid and be unable to settle short

term debts.

Otherwise, if it is too much money tied up in working capital, then it is move effectively and profitably by

investing in other assets.

Liquidity ratio = current assets/current liabilities

31 Oct 2010 liquidity ratio

$140 million/$140 million

=1

31 Oct 2009 liquidity ratio

$120 million/ $120 million

=1

Thus, it implies that Karachi has too little working capital, than it could become illiquid and be unable to settle

short term debts both these two years.

Q3 Cal. the following ratios for 2009 and 2010.

a. return on capital employed 31 Oct 2009 31 Oct 2010 $million $million

(Net profit/capital employed) x 100% (33/260) x100 (35/300) x100

= 12.69% = 11.67%

b. gross profit margin

(gross profit/sales turnover) x 100% (330-100)/330 x100 (400-120)/400x100

= 69.70% = 70%

c. net profit margin

(net profit/ sale turnover) x 100% (33/330) x 100 (35/400) x 100

= 10% = 8.75%

d. gearing

(long term loans/capital employed) x 100% (120/260) x100 (150/300) x100

= 46.15% = 50%

e. debtors days

(credit sale trade debtors/sale turnover) x 365 days (70/ 330) x 365 days (80 /400) x 365 days

= 77days = 73 days

Q4 On the basis of the ratios you have calculated, evaluate the change in performance

of Karachi paper products over the two years.

I shall evaluate what factors cause Karachi paper product plc to change in performance of these two years on the basis of these ratios analysis.

My evaluation aim of ratio analysis can indicate these results of Karachi product sale business to

whether it may continue invest in its business, whether it has ability to attract banks to lend more money,

whether what factors cause it's profiting is rising or falling and whether it's management is using resources efficiently.

Profit margin aims to assess how successful the management of business to has been reach to the paper products sale revenues (turnover) into both gross and net profits, it is used to measure performance of a company and management team.

It's gross profit margin is the same 70% of both of 2009 and 2010 years. It means that Sales turnover and cost of goods sold amount are increasing at the same level of both these two year.

However, it's net profit margin fell down 1.25% in 2010 year. It means that it shall spend more expenditure in 2010 year. I feel that it's management team performance is not efficient because who can't control expenditure effectively to cause it's net profit margin falling down, so who need to revise how to control expenditure spending .

Return on capital employed aims to assess profitability as primary efficiency ratio. The higher value of this ratio means the greater the return on capital invested in the business.

It's return on capital employed fell down 1.02% in 2010 year and it is 11.67%. It means that it's profitability is not high value to get the greater the return on capital invested. However, it can increase profit margin from these methods: By reducing paper product direct cost, e.g. cheaper material, relocation production to low labour cost countries, increasing productivity through automation in production or cutting wage cost by reducing workers' payment; by increasing paper sales price ; by reducing overhead cost, e.g. cutting

rent to move to a cheaper head office location and reducing promotion costs or management costs etc methods.

Liquidity means it assesses the ability of the firm to pay short term debts, it relates to working capital.

If there is too little working capital, then business could become illiquid and be unable to settle short

term debts. Otherwise, If it is too much money tied up in working capital, then it is move effectively and

profitably by investing in other assets. It's liquidity ratio is 1 both two years. It means that it's current assets

and current liabilities amount is the same. Although it's current assets amount is not less than current liabilities,

but if it's future current liabilities amount will increase, it's liquidity ratio will fall down to less than 1.

It is possible that it can become illiquid and be unable to settle short term debts. I recommend these methods to

increase liquidity : Selling fixed assets for cash and choosing to pay lease, e.g. land and property could be sold

to a leasing company; Selling old stocks (inventories) for cash, e.g. office furniture, office printers, fax

machines; Increasing loans to inject cash, e.g. issuing shares or borrowing long term loans.

Debtors days indicates short/long credit period to pay debts, it is no right or wrong result from business

to business and industry to industry. A high trade debtor days ratio may be a deliberate management

strategy, customers will be attracted to give extended credit, but poor control of debtors and repayment period. It has debtor days of 73 days and it reduced 4 days in 2010 year. It means it has no

high trade debtor days and customers will not be attracted to give extended credit easily.

Thus, it ought have more cash available and it ought to attempt to pay current liabilities to its creditors in these

two year.

Gearing ratio measures the degree to which capital of the business is finances from long term loans.

The greater is the reliance of a business on loan capital and the more highly geared.

The business gearing ratio gets result over 50%, it indicates a highly geared business and higher the

ratio and the greater risk is taken by shareholders to invest. Otherwise , a low gearing ratio, it indicates

a safe business strategy. Management is not borrowing to expand business. It can reduced ratio by increase

capital employed, such as issuing more shares or retaining profits.

It's gearing ratio is 50% and rises 3.85% in 2010 year. Although, it's gearing ratio doesn't reach to 50%, but

it will have greater risk is taken by shareholders to invest. Thus, I recommend it needs to issuing shares to

get capital source to reduce risk to shareholders to invest. Otherwise, shareholders will lose confidence to

invest to its business in the long term.

In conclusion, it's net profit margin is 8.75% and it fell down 1.25% and it is very low net profit income in 2010 and 2009 years. Although it's sales turnover is $400 million and it rises $70 million in 2010 year, but it's

gross profit margin is the same in these two years. Thus, if it still hope to do this business, it ought find what

the factors to cause it's net profit growth is not high, e.g. overspending expenditures, material cost increasing,

staffs expense increasing etc factors which influence it's income reduces. Otherwise, it will lose shareholders

confidence to invest to its business if they still earn less profit or loss in the future.

XXIV

manufacture management

Q1 Define the following terms:
a. flow production
Flow production producing items in a continually moving process, also known as line production.

This method is used when individual products move from stage to stage of the production process

as soon as the are ready, without having to wait for any other products. Flow products systems are

capable of producing large quantities of output in a relatively short time and so it suits industries

where demand for the product in question is high and consistent. It also suits the production of large

numbers of a standardization item that only requires minimal alternations.

b. job rotation

Job rotation is a system of moving people systemically , between a number of jobs and duties, is likely to be

the result of downsizing. This is because fewer people have the same number of jobs to do.

Q2 Analyse two disadvantages BMW may have encountered using flow production

Flow production producing items in a continually moving process, also known as line production.

This method is used when individual products move from stage to stage of the production process

as soon as the are ready, without having to wait for any other products. Flow products systems are

capable of producing large quantities of output in a relatively short time and so it suits industries

where demand for the product in question is high and consistent. It also suits the production of large

numbers of a standardization item that only requires minimal alternations.

BMW is one production of cars company, it's plant currently produces over 210,000 vehicles a year.

The first disadvantage BMW may encountered using flow production. The main disadvantage is the high

initial set up cost. By definition, capital intensive, high technology production lines are going to

cost a great deal of money.

As this method is used when individual products move from stage to stage of the production process

as soon as the are ready, without having to wait for any other products. Flow products systems are

capable of producing large quantities of output in a relatively short time. However, BMW needs to produce many vehicles and every vehicle needs many engines to prepare to produce from workmen

in every stage. Thus, it needs many large factories and employs many manufacturing workmen.

If any stages were occurred problem, it needed technical staffs to solve these problem, it should

extend long time to finish any vehicles to produce. It is possible that it could not budget to raise to produce

above 210,000 vehicle numbers within one year.

The second disadvantage is BMW manufacturing workmen should feel boring, de-motivating because

every manufacturing workmen needs to repetitive job to manufacture vehicles in every stage every day.

It is possible that they feel no interest and they can not increase to manufacture vehicles every day

efficiently.

Q3 Explain the characteristics of cell production

Cell production means spilling flow production into self contained groups that are responsible

for whole work units. For example, every cell does everything is responsible for organizing

work schedules, planning output, meeting order deadlines and quality from the cutting

and stitching processes in one footwear manufacturing company.

Thus, characteristics of cell production is a form of flow production, but instead of each individual worker

performing a single task, the production line is split into several self contained, mini-

production units-known as cell, Each individual cell produces a complete unit of work, such as a complete washing machine motor and not just a small part of it.

Each cell has a team leader and below that a single level of hierarchy made up of multi-

skilled workers. The performance of each cell is measured against pre-set targets.

These targets will include output level, quality and lead times. Cells are responsible for

the quality of their own complete units of work-this links in with total quality management

(TQM), job enrichment and team working .

Q4 Discuss the advantages and disadvantages to BMW of switching from flow production

to cell production.

The advantages and disadvantages to BMW of switching from flow production to cell

production as below:

On the disadvantages hand, BMW has used flow production method to manufacture vehicle for

a long time. If it decided to change to use from flow production method to cell production.

It's vehicle manufacturing workmen who needed spend much time to learn and to adapt how to

use cell production and who would not accept or rejected this cell production if they felt

difficult to adapt this cell production method.

On the advantages hand, flow production method can help BMW to move away from traditional

flow production to team based approach and the workforce was reorganized into self managing

teams or cells of between eight and 15 people. The teams can make production decisions and have job rotation schemes. Responsibility for achieving plant wide targets are now in the hands of those

teams. Each team has more of a stake in the way the business develops rather than a hierarchical

system where workers has decision making authority, initiative and leading to a dependency

culture. Thus, BMW achieve every team have authority to plan, decisions, suggestions and

points of view could be aired.

In conclusion, cell production method gives benefits to BMW to led to significant improvements

in worker commitment and motivation because there is team work and a sense of ownership

of the complete unit of car manufacturing work, job rotation within the cell and increased

productivity in possible. However, success of cell production depends on a well trained

and multi skilled workforce prepared and able to flexible and accept a more responsible

style or working.

XXV

product innovation

Q1 Define the following terms:

a. innovative products

Innovative products originate from the practical application of new inventions. They may have incurred

substantial research and development costs. They can result in substantial benefits to the business and to be

the country in which it operates. Some businesses are more likely than others to go through substantial

change by innovation, e.g. high technological computer products or pharmaceuticals.

b. trademarks

Trademarks are distinctive names, symbols or designs that identify a business or its products.

Trademarks can be legally registered and can't be copied.

Q2 Analyse the importance of companies such as Gillette continuing to spend large sums

on Research and development even in a global downturn.

The importance of companies such as Gillette continuing to spend large sums on research and

development, even in a global downturn.

The reasons it is important to spend large sums of research and development include:

(a) If it can innovate its fact beauty products successfully, then it can build women consumers'

confidence and raise its image and competitive position in this women face beauty products market.

(b) There are different types of face beauty products of which are innovated to manufacture to raise

quality to stay ahead of its competitors in global market. Hence, women consumers will have much choice to

compare all face beauty product prices and functions to decide to buy finally.

(c) In a global downturn environment, it must need to continue to innovate its face beauty products to

continue build its beauty products to continue build its customer loyalty to keep its competitive position.

Otherwise, global women clients must reduce to spend to buy any face beauty products.

(d) Spending research and development expenditure is a long term investment to innovate new

products for any company. So, Gillette is value to innovate its face beauty products to attempt to

raise sale premium prices because face beauty products need often innovate to raise its face beauty

products quality to give face health to women clients to increase their confidence. Even, it can reduce

lower costs to research and develop more health face beauty products for long term.

However, it has also reasons less important to spend large sums on research and development expenditure to

Gillette. as below:

(a) If Gillette's women face beauty products are manufactured to sell successfully, it means that its

existing products may have the potential to produce long term profit. However, before it decides to

innovate new face beauty products to spend too much time and research development and workers

employment expenditure. It ought to budget when it can get the benefit return back. Otherwise, it

would loss its research and development expenditure if it fails to research to innovate new face beauty

products.

(b) Gillette is a famous women face beauty products sale company. It's patents can protect designs

for set periods. So, it doesn't worry about that its client numbers will reduce seriously.

(c) For face beauty products, innovation may not be an important element to influence business income.

Other elements can include prices, quality, design, economy, clients' income level, clients' knowledge

of new product functions (benefits) to them, competitor numbers, advertisement methods, stores location

etc. Hence, it doesn't need only to concentrate on spending too much on how to improve face beauty

products innovation.

(e) Some innovations may not be patentable and so may be copied after high research and development

spending . Hence, Gillette's competitors may copy to attempt to innovate their other new face beauty

products from Gillette and they don't spend high research and development spending because some

Gillette's face beauty product innovations may not be patentable to sell in this face beauty products market.

In conclusion, Gillette ought need to attempt to research and develop to innovate new face beauty products,
even its competitors can attempt to copy its products because women clients prefer to choose to buy the
companies which can often innovate to promote new face beauty products. So, if it's face beauty
products are sold too long time and there are no any change. Clients will choose other competitors which
can often promote new face beauty products to attract them to buy in this face beauty product sale market.

XXVI

Management Calculation

Q1 Define the following terms:

a. mark up

This is the extra amount (usually a percentage added to costs of products or services when the sales

price is being set, e.g. 10% mark up would be cost plus 10% . (cost x 1.10) or (cost x 110/100).

b. variable cost

It means that business costs that vary with output changes of the year, such as materials used in

making a product or extra usages paid for extra time worked.

Q2 Using the cost information from the text, cal.

a. the full cost of the conference for the Friends of the General hospital

(including the equipment hire)

Cost of conference= variable cost x number of people + overhead allocation + equipment hire

= ($15 x100) + $1000 + $200

= $2700

Alternative calculation of conference cost = offered price + contribution paying hotel overheads

= $2200 + $500

=$2700

b. the price that the hotel would normally charge for a conference of this size with the equipment requested

Normal price = offered price + $1850

= $2200 + $1850

=$4050

Alternative calculation

Normal price = full cost of conference x 1.50

= $2700 x 1.50

= $4050

Q2 c. the profit the hotel would make at the normal price

profit at normal price = normal price of conference less cost of conference

= $4050 less $2700

= $1350

Q2 d. the contribution to the hotel's overheads and profit if the conference suite were let out for $2200.

(i) contribution costing means costing method that only allocates direct costs to cost/profit centres not

overhead costs.

(ii) contribution per unit means selling price of a product less variable costs per unit

(iii) contribution cost pricing means setting prices based on the variable costs of making a product in order to make a contribution towards fixed costs and profit.

contribution towards paying the hotel's overheads:

= price charged less (variable cost x number of people) less equipment hire cost

= $2200 - (15 x 4100) - $200

=$500

Q3 Using monetary and non monetary information evaluate Sheila Burns's decision to offer

the hospital the conference facilities at the reduced price.

The monetary information arguments evaluate Sheila Burn's decision to offer the hospital the conference

facilities at the reduced price.

On the positive hand, there will be a contribution towards the hotel's overheads which may not otherwise

have been made. At the end of February , alternative income may be unlikely. Although it could earn less

profit if Sheila's hotel decided to offer the conference facilities and rooms to the hospital client at the reduced

price, but it could help to get a possible source of future bookings and income in low season.

A loss may be possible to write off as a charitable contribution expense and so reduce the income tax charge

bill in this year.

On the negative hand, the influential people (hospital conferences facilities and conference rooms booking

clients) may expect the same deal for themselves or for their businesses if who ever want to hold a function

there in the future.

Speaking may reach other clients about the hotel discounted price and who might expect the same deal for themselves in the future.

By accepting the hospital client booking of reduced priced charged to conference service at the first time,

the hotel would lose the possible of making more contribution and profit if an alternative booking reduced

price charged to conference service would come for next time ,even more time.

The non monetary information arguments evaluate Sheila Burn's decision to offer the hospital the confidence

facilities at the reduced price.

On the positive hand, helping a worthy cause could enhance the hotel's good image to pubic if the hotel decided

to offer the hospital the confidence facilities at the reduced price, so public would believe it had enough capital

to do this hotel business long term and it was possible that future businesses were from contacts with influential

people, so the hotel's conference rooms and facilities booking hotel clients would help it to promote its

reduced price service charge to let their friends to know to raise its client numbers seriously.

Newspapers or magazines may report this hotel reduced price conference rooms and facilities booking service

news and this hotel's name may be mentioned, giving them free publicity to reduce to spend advertisement

expenditure for long term.

On the negative hand, existing clients may be angry that their loyalty is rewarded by higher price, so they

will feel unfair and they and their friends won't choose to use this hotel any service again.

In conclusion, this hotel could attempt to reduce price charge to booking conference facilities and rooms to this hospital client because it could still earn contribution profits if it charged this reduced service price to

this hospital and it was possible that this hospital influential people will help it to introduce this reduced

price service charge to their business friends to help it to increase business numbers seriously and conference

rooms and facilities booking service was not its main income source, it would not influence it's hotel rooms

and facilities service income seriously.

XXVII
production methods

Q1 Define the following terms:

a. batch production

It means producing a limited number of identical products , each item in the batch passes through

one stage of production before passing on to the next stage.

b. fixed cost

it means costs that do not vary with output in the short run, e.g. rent, depreciation

salary, electricity etc office expenditure.

Q2 Draw a break even chart for options 1 and 2 and show the break even points for each option.

(i) Break even chart includes the level of output at which total costs equal total revenue and

the amount of revenue needed to cover both fixed and variable costs so that the business breaks even.

windcheater car break even chart to produce roofrack products information:

current output capacity is at 5000 units per year
sale price of each roofrack $40
production costs of each roofrack
direct labour $10
direct material $12
fixed costs $54000
thus, per year income is 5000 x $40=$200,000
per year direct variable cost is 5000 x ($10+$12)=$110,000
per year fixed asset is $54000
break even level of output = fixed cost/ contribution per unit
= $54,000 / $40-$22
=3000 units

option 1 extending the existing premises, for expansion break event point is

current output capacity 5000 x 2 = 10,000 units per year
sale price of each roofrack $40
production costs of each roofrack
direct labour $10
direct material $12
fixed costs $54000 + $27000 =$81000
thus, per year income is $400,000
per year direct variable cost is 10,000 x ($10+$12)=$220,000
per year fixed asset is $81000
break even level of output = fixed cost/ contribution per unit
= $81000 / $40-$22
=4500 units
option 2 purchase new machinery, for expansion break event point is

current output capacity 5000 x 150%=7500 units
sale price per roofrack $40
production costs of each roofrack
direct costs = $12+$10-$2=$20
fixed costs $54000+$6000=$60000
thus , per year income is $ 7500 x $40=$300,000
per year direct variable cost is 7500 x $20=$150,000
per year fixed asset is $60,000
break even level of output = fixed cost/ contribution per unit
= $60000 / $40-$20
=3000 units

Q3 On the basis of your break even charts, explain which option Windcheater should choose.

The break even output of opinion 1 is 4500 units and opinion 2 is 3000 units and the margin of

safety is 3000 units if it does not choose to expand its output numbers.

If one company is producing below break even point, it is in danger. Although, option 2 break even

output numbers is same to margin of safety, but if it could not produce more output numbers to sell,

it is possible that it would be below than the margin of safety. However, opinion 1 break even output

numbers are more than 1500 units to margin of safety output numbers. Hence, it is more safe to

choose to expand to produce its output numbers, option 1 is choice.

Q4 Evaluate the usefulness of break even analysis to businesses like Windcheater.

The usefulness of break even analysis t businesses like Windcheater. Windcheater is motor accessory

shop. it uses batch production to produce its roofracks. Hence, it needs efficient method to help it to

evaluate whether how to make options to expand its output numbers is more suitable for long term.

If a business is able to calculate the break even quantity that must be sold to cover all costs, it will

be easier to make important production and marketing decisions.

Break event charts are relatively easy to construct and interpret for its business every option in the short

term, it provides useful guidelines to its management on break even points, safety margins and

profit/loss levels at different rates of output, comparisons can be made between different options by

constructing new charts to show changes circumstances. Thus , it can show the possible impact on

profit and break even point of a change in its output's selling price, the equation produces a precise

break even result and it can assist important decision, e.g. location decision, whether to buy new equipment

and which project to invest in and whether to extend the existing premise options.

However, assumption must not ensure right, e.g. it is also unlikely that fixed costs will remain

unchanged at different output levels up to maximum capacity, there is no allowance made for stock

levels on the break even chart and it is not actual occurrence for any business, it can not include

the semi variable cost and the assumption that costs and revenues are always representation

by straight lines is unrealistic.

However, in the short term options to make decision or new business investment decision to

decide whether which options are more suitable to produce more output numbers. Break even

chart is the best method to help business to make these decision.

XXVIII

Quality Ensure Measurement

Q1 Define the following terms:

a. quality assurance

Quality assurance is based on setting agreed quality standards to all stages in the production of a good or

service in order to ensure that client's satisfaction is achieved. It does not just focus on the finished product.

This approach often involves self-checking by workers of their own output against these agreed quality

standards.

b. continuous improvement

Continuous improvement is Japanese term meaning in role of Kaizen in quality management

The philosophy behind this idea is that all workers have something to contribute to improving

the way their business operates and the way the product is made. Traditional styles of management is possibly based on a Theory X approach, never give workers the opportunity to suggest improvement

to the way things are done because the assumption is that trained managers know best. The objective

of managers adopting this approach is to keep production up to the mark and then look for one off

improvements in the form of inventions or to make investments in machines to increase productivity.

Continuous improvement suggests workers actually know more than managers about how a job should be

done or how productivity might be improved. Someone who works at a task every day is actually

much more likely to know how to change it to improve either quality or productivity than a manager

with, perhaps, no hands on experience of production at all.

Another key feature of this idea is that improvement in productivity don't just result from massive

one off investment in new technology. A series of small improvements, suggested by staff teams, can

over time, amount to as big an improvement in efficiency as a major new investment.

Q2 Outline two drawbacks to this business of not meeting customer expectations.

Fat Boy Trims is one haircutting and styling service company, it have more branches at different locations.

If it still not meeting customer expectations, it will cause these two drawbacks to this business.

Currently , the number of complaints received at head office about the branch and the quality of its

haircutting and styling services has been much greater than for any other location. It's revenues had fallen and the number of repeat customers had also fallen.

As a consequence, its branch had spent more on advertising for new business than any other. The revenue per

client was also low as high value services. , such as colouring and tinting were avoided by clients.

Its old clients can choose to find its competitors to help them to do hair cutting etc service, it will cause to

close its business as possible.

Q3 Analyze the benefits to this hairdressers of improving the quality of their service.

The benefits to this hairdresser of improving the quality of their service include:

It can makes every branches and its main shop haircutters responsible for hair cutting service

quality, this can be a form of job enrichment.

Every hair cutter can be self checking and making efforts to improve their hair cutting skills and

service attitude to increase motivation.

The system can be used to trace back service quality problems to the stage of the hair cutting

service process where a problem might have occurring.

Q4 Discuss the problems the new manager of FatBoyTrims might have when trying to implement the quality

targets she has set.

The problems the new manager of FatBoyTrims might have when trying to implement the quality

targets she has set include:

She set quality targets for each stage of the customer experience, e.g. maximum time for phone to ring, maximum waiting time for appointment time, maximum time between hair wash and cutting, all customers

to be offered refreshments, minimum time spent by stylists with each client and feedback forms to be

filled by 20% of clients and stylists responsible for each client to discuss answers with client.

Each member of staff was given responsibility for at east one of these targets in an attempt to achieve

continuous improvement in the hairdressers. A record had to be kept of the branch's success at meeting

these targets.

At first, branch costs increased as an additional staff member has to be recruited to help meet the

quality standards. Although, after four months, revenue has climbed by 38% and increasing client

satisfaction. It means that it need to spend more employment expenditure to help this manager to care

client hair cutting service need in every branch for long term. Every member will feel more job to done

and increase pressure to work if every branch hair cutter numbers are not enough, who shall leave whose

employer to choose to work to another new hair cutting employer if she can not increase whose salary.

If it expanded more branches , she can not manage many branches efficiently by herself alone. She needs

branch assistant managers to help her to deal any branch complains.

Hence, her quality targets won't be achieved possibly if this haircutting shop can not give professional

hair cutting skill training to new hair cutters and old hair cutters and she has no assistant managers to share her job responsibilities in every branches and these staffs salary ought to be raised to let

its professional hair cutters and counter service staffs feel fair treatment in this hair cutting market.

XXIX

Joint venture

Q1 define the following terms:

a. joint venture

This is a separate legal entity set up by two or more other businesses, combining their expertise and

sharing the costs, control, risk and eventual profits/ losses. For example, mining and energy two different

projects join together to do business. Thus, it can describe a variety of business arrangements involving

two or more parties pursuing a joint undertaking with a view to mutual benefit.

An unincorporated joint venture is essentially a business relationship in which the participants hold the joint

venture property as tenants in common rather than through ownership of a corporate entity which owns the

join venture property. It is a legal relationship to which the law of contract applies and it can be created by

conduct verbally or in any number of documents, but the key terms and conditions of the joint venture

relationship should be set out in a written agreement.

b. import duties

These are taxes due when importation of products passes through a national boundary between countries

or trading. It is usually based on the sales price of the item.

Q2 Explain two qualitative factors Mercedes might take into account when choosing to locate in Cairo.

The crisis on the Automotive manufacturing industry in developing countries because of any company

location of assembly and plants in national and regional production systems, the effects of the crisis have been

largely have been contained within each country/ regions.

Before, Mercedes makes any decisions about the best country in which locates new vehicles manufacturing

plants, it must evaluate many alternatives and factors involving international location decisions.

These factors are different according to types and size and location of parent company and geographical

areas of business.

However ,the two qualities factors Mercedes might take into account when choosing to locate in Cairo.

The motivation of Mercedes seeking to manufacture vehicles abroad reasons:

Mercedes is a German vehicles manufacturing company which chooses to locate in Germany, Cairo.

Cairo is a good market location to develop automotive manufacturing business because centrally

designed vehicles are manufacturing in multiple regions and Mercedes can build buyer-supplier

relationship in production regions and because of deep investments in capital equipment and skills, regional automotive clusters tend to be very long lived. So, whether Cairo is a large extent due to

the close relations with its suppliers and convenient transportation in particular the geography factor of

Mercedes shall consider.

Access to low cost input factors which refers to labour, material, capital and components and in order to

maximise profitability on manufacturing costs. For example, evaluating differences in operating costs,

as well as quality of life factors for each location. For example, availability of a quality workforce and

favourable business climate are likely to be important factors for automotive assembly plants at this

stage in the selection process.

Thus, for automobile manufacturing industry, comparing locations of production and organizational units ,

e.g. transportation cost, rentals, wages links to environment expenditures are the main factors to determine

of location and financial profits are not the only determinant of location.

Access to local vehicles manufacturing technological resources.

Proximity to markets, which results in faster and better client service. For example, a food processing

plant may view proximity to output markets as being a primary factor in the site choice.

Less industrial threats occur in Cairo, as companies seek to serve international markets, these have been a

growing number of manufacturing plants located on a world wide basis. International manufacturing is one of the major parts of a firm's competitive strategy. In conclusion, to sum up the complex economic geography of the automotive industry. Production tends to be organized regionally or nationally, with bulky, heavy and model specific parts production concentrated close to final assembly plants to assure timely delivery. Germany, Cairo is one good industrialized developing country to provide local levels for open factories to manufacture cars for operational reasons, such as just in time production to support of global produced vehicle platform.

Q3 Analyse the two reasons why Mercedes chose to use a joint venture when entering the Egyptian economy.

The two reasons why Mercedes chose to use a joint venture when entering the Egyptian location in Germany include:

Reason one: Assembling cars need Mercedes expertise and standards.

Entrepreneurs would probably not be able to assemble Mercedes parts to Mercedes standards with Mercedes guidance if which have no joint venture with Mercedes, Mercedes needs to be directly involved with ensuring standards of their name is to used to sell cars in Egyptian Germany market, Mercedes have expertise in manufacturing, so know how to go about controlling the process to cooperate with other entrepreneurs to manufacture cars efficiently and easily.

However, the entrepreneurs and Mercedes joint venture also have these disadvantages:

The entrepreneurs may wish to lower standards in order to make profit if they chose to be joint venture with

Mercedes, Germany local workforce may not be used to working to such high standards, Germany 45%

locally car manufactured parts are required, so it will need more than just imported parts to manufacture cars.

Reason two: local rules and regulations need local experts in Germany

Germany local entrepreneurs may know local rules better more than Mercedes, so Mercedes and Germany

local entrepreneurs join venture to open factory to manufacture cars in Germany ; the Germany local

entrepreneurs must give Germany employment law and business law regulation to let Mercedes to

manufacture cars business in Germany easily ; local entrepreneurs may have important local contracts

and influence to build suppliers and client relationship more than Mercedes, so Mercedes choose to join

venture with Germany local entrepreneurs which can help it to build this car manufacturing business easily;

local entrepreneurs may be move in touch with drastic and sudden changes in requirements in Germany,

so, Mercedes choose to join venture with Germany entrepreneurs which can help it to do its business in

this strange country more easily.

However, the entrepreneurs and Mercedes joint venture also have these disadvantages:

Mercedes needs to trust local entrepreneurs not to take advantage of Mercedes, Mercedes needs to share

profits with the local entrepreneurs in Germany and local rules can change faster than it is easy to adapt to

do car manufacturing business in Germany.

In conclusion, Mercedes ought attempt to choose joint venture with other entrepreneurs to manufacture car sale business in Germany because it is its first time to open factory to manufacture cars to sell in Germany.

It can build local suppliers and clients relationship and local manufacturing requirement in Germany easily

if Germany other entrepreneurs are its competitors. Otherwise if they can co-operate to do car manufacturing

sale business in Germany, Mercedes must earn long term benefits from their help.

Q4 Discuss the advantages and disadvantages to Mercedes of expanding into the developing economies

like Egypt.

Developing economies means that the countries' economies are developing in industrialization process,

e.g. Germany is one developing country for benefits to manufacturing industry development .

Thus, Germany economy is slow development, not only with regard to the speed of the development

(the rate of industrial growth) , but also with regard to the productive and organizational structures of

industry with emerged from those processes. For example, the idea is that Germany's industrialization

would be different from Britain's due to timing because these two countries' economy which are

developing in different time. Nowadays, Germany is one industrialized developing economic country.

Otherwise, British is a developed economic country, it doesn't depend on industrial manufacturing , it

economic development is depended on service industry.

The advantages and disadvantages to Mercedes, German Automation car manufacturing company of

expanding into developing economies like Egypt in Germany as below:

On the advantages hand, Mercedes expands to open factories to expand its car manufacturing sale market in Germany.

Germany can provide local cheaper labour to Mercedes factories, Mercedes can rent or buy cheaper land to build factories to manufacture car for long term in Germany, Germany is a developing industrialized country.

It is faster expanding market to compare to choose to open factories to manufacture car in developed countries, thus Germany is high potential profits country in car sale industry, Germany Government can charge lower profit tax to local business.

On the disadvantages hand, Mercedes lacks of local supplier contracts and close relationships with them and manufacturing car knowledge and local requirement and law to open factories to do car manufacturing business in Germany, cultural differences may make operations more difficult with Mercedes ' country manufacturing car culture, differences in Germany local standards may challenge Mercedes car manufacturing company standards and Mercedes lacks of adequately skilled local employees if it decides to open factories to manufacture cars in Germany.

However, Germany is one industrialized developing country, it can give more benefits to Mercedes to open factories to manufacture cars to sell in Germany. Mercedes can attempt to expand this car sales market.

XXX

Innovation Advantages

Q1 Define the following terms:

a. innovative products

Innovative products originate from the practical application of new inventions. They may have incurred

substantial research and development costs. They can result in substantial benefits to the business and to be

the country in which it operates. Some businesses are more likely than others to go through substantial

change by innovation, e.g. high technological computer products or pharmaceuticals.

b. trademarks

Trademarks are distinctive names, symbols or designs that identify a business or its products.

Trademarks can be legally registered and can't be copied.

Q2 Explain how the use of innovative products and

trademarks can add to the value of a company
such as Gillette.

The value of a company is investment when either the capital employed is boosted by retained
earnings or share prices raise the market value.

The use of innovative products and trademarks can add to the value of a company
such as Gillette.

Its trademarks can be famous to public and its trademarks can be as a goodwill to let women to
believe Gillette's women face beauty products quality is preferable. It means that Gillette's
innovative face beauty products' trademarks can raise its sale income and growth value for
long term.

This can occur because innovation differentiates Gillette from competitors, if it could
innovate its face beauty products to let women clients accept more in the market.

It can keep ahead of the competition to raise it's trademarks image to global clients to believe
that it often innovate to research new face beauty health products to women.

Q3 Analyse the importance of companies such as Gillette continuing to spend large sums
on Research and development even in a global downturn.

The importance of companies such as Gillette continuing to spend large sums on research and
development, even in a global downturn.

The reasons it is important to spend large sums of research and development include:

(a) If it can innovate its fact beauty products successfully, then it can build women consumers'
confidence and raise its image and competitive position in this women face beauty products market.

(b) There are different types of face beauty products of which are innovated to manufacture to raise
quality to stay ahead of its competitors in global market. Hence, women consumers will have much choice to
compare all face beauty product prices and functions to decide to buy finally.

(c) In a global downturn environment, it must need to continue to innovate its face beauty products to
continue build its beauty products to continue build its customer loyalty to keep its competitive position.
Otherwise, global women clients must reduce to spend to buy any face beauty products.

(d) Spending research and development expenditure is a long term investment to innovate new
products for any company. So, Gillette is value to innovate its face beauty products to attempt to
raise sale premium prices because face beauty products need often innovate to raise its face beauty
products quality to give face health to women clients to increase their confidence. Even, it can reduce
lower costs to research and develop more health face beauty products for long term.

However, it has also reasons less important to spend large sums on research and development expenditure to
Gillette. as below:

(a) If Gillette's women face beauty products are manufactured to sell successfully, it means that its
existing products may have the potential to produce long term profit. However, before it decides to

innovate new face beauty products to spend too much time and research development and workers

employment expenditure. It ought to budget when it can get the benefit return back. Otherwise, it

would loss its research and development expenditure if it fails to research to innovate new face beauty

products.

(b) Gillette is a famous women face beauty products sale company. It's patents can protect designs

for set periods. So, it doesn't worry about that its client numbers will reduce seriously.

(c) For face beauty products, innovation may not be an important element to influence business income.

Other elements can include prices, quality, design, economy, clients' income level, clients' knowledge

of new product functions (benefits) to them, competitor numbers, advertisement methods, stores location

etc. Hence, it doesn't need only to concentrate on spending too much on how to improve face beauty

products innovation.

(e) Some innovations may not be patentable and so may be copied after high research and development

spending . Hence, Gillette's competitors may copy to attempt to innovate their other new face beauty

products from Gillette and they don't spend high research and development spending because some

Gillette's face beauty product innovations may not be patentable to sell in this face beauty products market.

In conclusion, Gillette ought need to attempt to research and develop to innovate new face beauty products, even its competitors can attempt to copy its products because women clients prefer to choose to buy the

companies which can often innovate to promote new face beauty products. So, if it's face beauty

products are sold too long time and there are no any change. Clients will choose other competitors which

can often promote new face beauty products to attract them to buy in this face beauty product sale market.

Q4 Evaluate the factors that determine the level of innovation in an industry.

Innovation definition is the introduction of a new product , service or process through a

certain business model into the marketplace, is either by utilization or by commercialization.

Hence, it includes product innovation, service innovation , process innovation and business

model innovation and all contribution to strengthen the competitive advantage of certain company.

The factors that determine the level of innovation in an industry which include external and internal

factors to affect the product and business process innovation.

External factors include industry maturity, customer needs and expectations, technological

opportunities, investment attractiveness, intensity of competition, company size,

origin of ownership and export orientation.

Internal factors include company requires developing new competences and routines to help

product innovation, knowledge and resource and human capital and equipments and capital input elements

etc.

XXXI

Capacity Increasing Methods

Q1 Define the following terms:

a. increase in capacity

This is a rise in the maximum level often production of a product supported by the manufacturing facilities.

Usually a business will want to produce to increase capacity utilisation, this will allow fixed cost to be as

thinly spread as possible. It means that unit costs are as low as possible. So, in order to measure the use of

capacity , a firm must measure its capital utilisation by actual output is divided by capacity multiple of

100%.

For example, there may be occasions of a top manufacturer needs to produce more than their normal capacity levels before public holiday, there are a number of ways , such as changing shift pattern,

e.g. more hours are worked than normal, longer opening hours,, e.g. shops at holiday, employing

temporary workers, e.g. the post office at holiday, overtimes, this is usually paid at a higher rate

than normal.

b. increase in scale of operation

This is a rise in the size of the business inputs and resources . It may refer to capacity , but if may

also refer to elements, such as the size of the (employees) workforce, value of turnover, assets employed,

capital employed, profit level of firms and stock market value of companies.

Thus, there is no ideal business size, each business must find the size most suitable for its operations.

However, the increase in economies of scale (sale of operation) can be achieved in five ways, such as

marketing, financial, managerial, technical and purchase ways.

c. no buffer stock

This means that all existing supplies (inventories) are used up when supplies (inventories) are

scheduled to arrive, so there is no safety margin in case the new supplies arrive late. It implies any

business warehouses (stores) can no excess stocks (supplies) to keep in them if existing inventory

numbers are calculated to used or sold budget numbers as soon as possible.

Q2 Explain the difference between stock holding costs and the costs of not

holding enough stock

Stock holding costs are the costs of having stock when the business may not need it for production.

For example: storage cost, stock handling costs, loss and damage of stock, opportunity cost etc.

The cost of not holding stocks are the potential disadvantages of not having stock, for example:

. Unexpected orders may not be able to be filled.

. Production stops in supplies run out.

.Special orders could be difficult/ experience to produce.

.Raw material orders may be small , so the company would lose out on potential purchasing economies.

Q3 Analyze two criteria MFLEX needs to meet in order to use JIT stock

management successfully.

Just in time stock management, means just in time. It is a stock control method that originated in

Japan and aim to avoid holding stocks by requiring supplies to arrive just as they are needed for

production completed products are produced only to order and for immediate delivery.

Criteria may include:

. Close relationships and communication with suppliers and clients.

.Flexible production staff able to switch between production of different products.

.Machines able to produce large batches, then switch products.

. Accurate computerised demand forecasting can be expensive.

. Excellent employer - employee relationships.

.Quality must be right first time as there is no stock to fall back on cost of halting production if supplies don't arrive must not be greater than the cost of holding stocks.

. Low inflation does not mean that stock holding is a way of beating inflation.

MFLEX is one electronic product sales company, it's characteristics of just in time systems needs to

focus on reducing inefficiency and unproductive time in the production process to improve continuously

the process and the quality of the product or service.

Employee involvement and inventory reduction are essential to just in time operations to aims to achieve

zero inventory, stockless production.

For example, Mc Donald's fast food restaurant, there are two workstations. the burger maker is the person

responsible for producing this burger food: Burger patties must be fried, buns must be toasted and then

dressed with ketch up, lettuce and cheese food must be inserted into buns and put on a tray.

The final assembler takes the tray , wraps the burgers in paper and restocks the inventory.

Inventories must be kept low because any burgers left unsold after seven minutes must be destroyed.

One way to manage this flow is by using the push method, in which the production of the item begins in

advance of client needs. With this method, management schedules the receipt of all raw materials e.g.

meat, buns etc food and authorizes the start of production.

The burger maker starts production of 24 burgers (the capacity) and when they are completed,

pushes them along to the final assembler's station, where they might have to wait until who is ready for them. The packages burgers then wait on a warning tray until a client purchases one.

Firms that tend to have highly repetitive manufacturing processes and well defined material flows

use just a time material because the pull method allows closer control of inventory and production at

the workstations. Other firms , such as those products in low values with low repeatability in the

production processes, delivery on some future date. In this case, client order is promised for delivery on some

future date. production is started at the first workstation and pushed ahead to the next one. Inventory can

accumulate at each workstation because workstations are responsible for producing many other orders and

may be busy at any particular line.

It can eliminated production line inspectors and cut the number of supervisors by itself.

For example. Mc Donald's has two high or too low stock takes risk because high stocks represent money

lying idle when it could be put to better use, whereas low stocks could result in not and satisfy clients needs.

Problem of low stocks include:

It may be difficult to satisfy guests' demands, it can led to a loss of business goodwill, ordering needs to be

frequent and handling costs are higher.

There is an increased risk of a stock item became obsolete, the risk of stock losses is increased,

the costs of storage are high, stocks can tie up a company's working capital.

Q4 Evaluate MFLEX's decision to use JIT stock management.

MFLEX's decision to use JIT stock management, it is centralized stock management system benefits include:

. Avoiding out of stock, the accurate level of stock is simply input currently onto the system. As a result,

clients can always get that they order.

. Avoiding reduced automatically at the end of a promotion.

. Stock levels are always optimum to ensure sales and the updated electronic products.

. stock levels are always optimum to ensure sales .

.Cost saving results from less waste and passes on value for clients.

. Time saving is as ordering bases on the level of current stocks which is already shown on the system.

.Cost reduction, budget will not be tied up but can be used .

. Areas are in obviously used to store, can be used for other more.

. Higher quality of electronic products, the used electronic material is updates resulting less waste and greater

client satisfaction.

Positive: customers are demanding just in time stock management to MFLEX, close relationships and

communication with suppliers and clients already exists exclusive deals signed and computer links will

speed up communication, new factory may not have room for storage or storage could cot more.

Negative: rapid inflation and rising cost of components, higher transport charges more expensive

for frequent small orders and problems delivering supplies could cause costly halts in production.

In conclusion , MFLEX's decision to use JIT stock management, just in time is only purchase enough

electronic material each day to produce waits as actual clients demand or raw material are received

just in time to get into production and units are completed just in time to be served to clients.

Hence, just in time management can give benefits to MELEX electronic manufacturing include that

it can meet time and product expectation and specification to deliver enough different models of electronic

products to shops to sell to clients from stores, it can raise advanced electronic products quality assurance and

delivery electronic products quality, lead time, it can raise store administrative stock record accuracy and

it can reduce overhead costs , e.g. more store space capacity, less delivery expense, less electricity charge,

less warehouse rent etc expense.

XXXII

Private Limited Companies Strategies

Q1 Define the following terms:

a. Private limited company

It is a small to medium sized business that is owned by shareholders who are often members of

same family. This company can not sell shares to the general public.

b. project management

It uses modern management techniques to carry out and complete a project

from start to finish in order to achieve pre-set targets of quality, time and cost.

For example, setting up a new information technological system, relocation company operations, installing machinery, developing and launching a new product, building a factory etc business projects.

Q2 Based on the information on the factory closure:

a. construct a network diagram for closing the factory

Network diagram means the diagram used in critical path analysis that shows the logical sequence

of activities and the logical dependencies between them and the critical path can be identified.

Jamaica photos is one firm specialises in photographic processing and it operates in two sites.

Closing factory activities

Activity Description duration Days preceding activites

A End processing in Montego,run down stocks of 2 - materials

B Dismantle machinery 4 A

C Knock out doorway to allow machinery to be moved 2 A

D pack office equipment 2 A

E Transportation 3 B,C,D

F suspend processing at Kingston 8 -

G Assemble machinery transported from Montego 3 E

H Re organise production facilities in kingston 2 E

I Test new integrated processing system 2 G,H

Activities logical sequence to close factory

F (8 days)

Suspend processing

B (4 days) G (3days)

dismantle machinery Assemble machinery

A (2 days) transportation

End processing, I(2 days)

run down stocks of C(2 days) test new

materials knock out doorway to E(3 days) H(2 days)

processing
allow machinery to be moved Transportation Re-organize
system
production facilities
  D (2 days)
Pack office equipment

b. cal. the ESTs and LFTs for each activity
  It needs to complete the task within 15 working days if
teams can get bonus.
  Earliest start time means earliest possible point time on
which a task can start based on predecessor connections.
  EST (Earliest start time) of tasks with no predecessors =
First logical starting point.
EST of tasks with predecessors = predecessor EFT
  Latest finishing time means later possible in time on
which a task can in time without causing
  a delay in the overall timeline.
  EST LFT
Activity Activity
A =0 days 2days
B =2 6
C =2 4
D =2 4
E =3 10
F =0 8
G =11 14
H =13 15
I =16 21
  c. identify the critical path
  Critical path means the sequence of activities that must
be completed on time for the whole project
  to be completed by the agreed date.

The F must not critical path because F has no preceding activities, it is suspend processing at Kingston

Activities B,C,D is preceding to activity E, and activity activities G, H must precede to activity I .

thus, other activities are critical path to complete to end of activity I.

The critical path does not include F

Q3 Evaluate the usefulness of critical path analysis to the management of Jamaica photos

Critical path analysis means planning technique that identifies all tasks in a project , puts them

in the correct sequence and allows for the identification of the critical path. It provides four

key respects:

.To estimate overall project duration.

.To create a logical sequence of project tasks.

. To track project progress and identify potential delays.

. To identify potential fast track possibilities.

However, it relies on a four simple assumptions to Jamaica photos :

. Closing factory and moving equipment to new site project is made up of tasks.

. Tasks are combined to form a timeline.

.Within this timeline, tasks are either concurrent or sequential (one task can't begin until

the predecessor)

.Sequential dependent tasks make up the critical path.

Critical path management is helpful in Jamaica photos to reduce time cost to move equipments to

close factory. Operational resources are expensive and the most expensive resource is that which is unused or underused, unused stocks take up space and working capital; machinery left idle wastes capital

and can require protective maintenance; labour waiting for supplies to arrive will add unnecessarily

to the wages bill. Efficient firm will always aim to use their resources as intensively as possible

and avoid wasted time and idle assets. Keeping assets busy is not always as easy as project is

a complex one.

XXXIII

Diseconomic of Scale

Q1 Define the following terms:
a. diseconomies of scale
Diseconomies of scale mean there are negative factors that make operations more experience or less
efficient as a business grows. They may include internal and/or external factors. Internal factors may
include reduce control or co-ordination less efficient communication, deterioration in working
relationships with a larger organization, increased bureaucracy. External factors may include land
scarcity and an increase in prices of the many businesses locate in one area, lack of qualified workers
and transport congestion. Factors that cause average costs of production to rise when the scale of operation is
increased.
It is occurred at the short term in the beginning of any business. For long term, scale of operation

may be achieved because the maximum output that can be achieved using the available inputs

(resources), it can increased in the long term by employing more of all inputs.

b. joint venture

This is a separate legal entity set up by two or more other businesses, combining their expertise and

sharing the costs, control, risk and eventual profits/ losses. For example, mining and energy two different

projects join together to do business. Thus, it can describe a variety of business arrangements involving

two or more parties pursuing a joint undertaking with a view to mutual benefit.

An unincorporated joint venture is essentially a business relationship in which the participants hold the joint

venture property as tenants in common rather than through ownership of a corporate entity which owns the

join venture property. It is a legal relationship to which the law of contract applies and it can be created by

conduct verbally or in any number of documents, but the key terms and conditions of the joint venture

relationship should be set out in a written agreement.

Q2 produce a SWOT analysis for Walmart's decision to expand into India.

SWOT analysis means a forms of strategic analysis that identifies and analyses the main internal

strengths and weaknesses and external opportunities and threats that will influence the future direction

and success of a business.

On internal strengths hand, Walmart has an established office in India which can do market research, strategic analysis, long experience and internal experience, access to large amounts of capital.

On internal weakness hand, diseconomies of scale when expand to India from head office, lack of

core competence which allow them of differentiate themselves.

On the external opportunities hand, India is one potential market and second most populated country

in the world, it has 200 million middle income consumers, its market not saturated, its legal restrictions

may be dropped, Walmart retail warehouse (supermarket) can be joint venture with local companies to

co-operate to do cheap price product sale business to prevent foreign retailers to enter India market from

owning shops.

On the external threats hand, Indian tradition of buying from stores and market trader competitors are

existing in India cheaper retail products sale market, local competition is reliance of local supermarkets

exist in India and Walmart lacks weak supply chain local suppliers to help it to deliver its groceries to

different Walmart warehouses areas in India efficiently.

Q3 Use Porter's five forces model to analyse the business environment Walmart will encounter in

India if it is allowed to open its own retail stores.

Michael Porter provided a framework that analyses an industry as being influenced by five forces.

It has been suggested that management, attempting to establish a competitive marketing advantage

over competitors, can use this model to understand the industry context in which the business operates and take appropriate strategic decision. I shall indicate the five forces include threat of entry, the power

of buyers, the power of suppliers, the threat of substitutes and competitive competitors(rivalry) to analyze

the business environment Walmart will encounter in India if it is allowed to open its own retail stores.

The threat of new entrants: Although ,local business have fewer restrictions in entering the cheap retailing

market to India, but it is not easy for a local business to enter this market as it requires significant capital to

open hypermarkets in India ; The longer it takes Walmart to gain Government clearance, the more likely that

local businesses may be better prepared to be first to open a hypermarket (cheap retailing warehouse). Thus,

Walmart competition will increase in India market.

The buyer power: Local buyers traditionally prefer small retailers and local market of their buying

behaviour choice stalls in India.

Threat of substitutes: This doesn't mean substitute products in the same industry, it refers to substitute

products in other industries. In the food supply industry it could, for example, mean extension of online

business to supply groceries. This is not mentioned in the case study. Thus, it is possible there are online

groceries supplies to use online sale method to provide clients more groceries purchase choice.

Competitive rivalry: This is a combination of the other four factors and it sums up the whole picture.

Power of suppliers: India lack enough suppliers to help Walmart to deliver its groceries to different

warehouses in India areas. Thus, It lacks of supporting local infrastructure in India, India has weak supply

chains to support Walmart groceries retailing business development.

Q4 Evaluate Walmart's strategy of expanding into emerging economy markets.

Emerging economy means there are countries in the world that are experiencing fast growth and

industrialisation.

Walmart's strategy of expanding into emerging economy markets, it can get these advantages possibly.

It can earn potential profits, India is a non saturated cheap groceries (products) sale market. India is

an emerging economic country, it is experiencing fast growth and industrialisation stage and it is less

compensation to compare with other countries. So potentially greater margins to be made. There are few

alternatives left for expansion for very big international companies in India. Walmart can pay lower cost,

e.g. land and labour to open its warehouses in India different areas. India Government may give incentives

in tax breaks or grants to assist overseas business investors and less restrictive laws.

Although, India is a emerging economic country to experience fast growth and industrialization, it has

also these disadvantages: It lacks of supporting local infrastructure in India, India has weak supply chains to

support Walmart groceries retailing business development. It is possible that Walmart will encounter communication problem because Walmart head office is at America. Its staffs need long time to communicate

to its Walmart retailing warehouses staffs in India, even its India and America staffs will have cultural and

language difference to cause conflict during they need to discuss in meeting possibly.

India local law will restrict foreign ownership to invest in India possibly and Walmart substantial investment

needed prior to being able to start to compare further new retailing groceries sale competitors entering to

India market. Thus, it need to spend long time to build its brand to let Indian to know what its products will

sell in India.

In conclusion, although India has much risk to threaten Walmart to invest its groceries retailing to

India market ,e.g. there will have more online similar groceries product businessmen choose to sell

cheap groceries by online shopping to India market.

However, India is one emerging economic country. It is experiencing fast growth and industrialization.

Walmart is one USA famous large discount groceries retailing warehouse company to earn profit in

itself country market and it's USA market has reached to saturated.

Walmart strategy expanding to another country new market, India. It is fast growth and industrialization

and India Government will encourage overseas businessmen to develop their businesses to invest in its

country because India will reduce unemployment, Government will increase tax income etc benefits

from overseas investment . Hence, Walmart ought attempt to invest another new overseas market to sell its groceries products to increase its client numbers and profits , even if India market development can earn

profits , then Walmart can continue to develop other new countries' markets to raise its client numbers for

long term.